Clause and Effect

Springer
Berlin
Heidelberg
New York
Barcelona
Budapest
Hongkong
London
Mailand
Paris
Santa Clara
Singapur
Tokio

William F. Clocksin

Clause
and Effect

Prolog Programming
for the Working Programmer

 Springer

Dr. William F. Clocksin
Computer Laboratory
University of Cambridge
Pembroke Street
Cambridge CB2 3QG, UK

Computing Reviews Classification (1991): D.1.6

Library of Congress Cataloging-in-Publication Data

Clocksin, W. F. (William F.), 1955–
    Clause and effect: Prolog programming for the working programmer
/ William F. Clocksin.
        p. cm.
    Includes bibliographical references and index.
    ISBN 3-540-62971-8 (pbk.: alk. paper)
    1. Prolog (Computer program language)
QA76.73.P76C565   1997
005.13'--dc21   97-35795
                                                           CIP

ISBN 3-540-62971-8 Springer-Verlag Berlin Heidelberg New York

© Springer-Verlag Berlin Heidelberg 1997
Printed in Germany

Cover Design: Künkel + Lopka Werbeagentur, Heidelberg
Typesetting: Camera ready by the author
SPIN 10574132   45/3142 – 5 4 3 2 1 0 – Printed on acid-free paper

Preface

This book is for people who have done some programming, either in Prolog or in a language other than Prolog, and who can find their way around a reference manual.

The emphasis of this book is on a simplified and disciplined methodology for discerning the mathematical structures related to a problem, and then turning these structures into Prolog programs. This book is therefore not concerned about the particular features of the language nor about Prolog programming skills or techniques in general. A relatively pure subset of Prolog is used, which includes the 'cut', but no input/output, no assert/retract, no syntactic extensions such as if-then-else and grammar rules, and hardly any built-in predicates apart from arithmetic operations. I trust that practitioners of Prolog programming who have a particular interest in the finer details of syntactic style and language features will understand my purposes in not discussing these matters.

The presentation, which I believe is novel for a Prolog programming text, is in terms of an outline of basic concepts interleaved with worksheets. The idea is that worksheets are rather like musical exercises. Carefully graduated in scope, each worksheet introduces only a limited number of new ideas, and gives some guidance for practising them. The principles introduced in the worksheets are then applied to extended examples in the form of case studies.

Clause and Effect can be a useful companion to two other books. The beginner might use *Clause and Effect* as a sequel to the introductory text *Programming in Prolog*. The more experienced programmer may start with *Clause and Effect* and be writing useful programs within a few hours. This book also conforms to ISO Standard Prolog, and it may be beneficial to use the reference manual *Prolog: The Standard* in conjunction with this book. Details of the other books are:

> *Programming in Prolog*, by W.F. Clocksin and C.S. Mellish. 4th edition. Springer-Verlag, 1994. ISBN 3-540-58350-5.
>
> *Prolog: The Standard*, by P. Deransart, A. Ed-Dbali, and L. Cervoni. Springer-Verlag, 1996. ISBN 3-540-59304-7.

Provided that the reader is equipped with a Prolog implementation that conforms to the ISO standard, the book *Prolog: The Standard* almost obviates the need for an implementation-specific reference manual, although the latter would be useful for documenting implementation-defined parameters and limits.

Since the publication in 1971 of Saunders MacLane's textbook on category theory, *Categories for the Working Mathematician*, book titles of the form 'X for the Working Y' have appealed to a number of authors. By using the same form as a subtitle, I hope that *Clause and Effect: Prolog Programming for the Working Programmer* will be not only of interest to those on the way to learning Prolog, but will also provide some visions of how Prolog might be applied to tasks of interest to those engaged with practical applications. For those with some experience of practical programming, I hope this book will provide a compact and refreshing approach with a distinctive style. But above all, I aim to show that programming in Prolog can be creative and fun.

Acknowledgements

This book has emerged from material prepared for courses I have taught at the University of Cambridge. Some of that material was based on notes that Chris Mellish and I made while giving short courses on Prolog to commercial firms in the early 1980s. I thank Chris for his involvement with the origins of techniques for rapid training in the use of Prolog. I thank the generations of students on whom this book was tested in its successive formats as lecture notes. I am indebited to my colleagues Martin Richards, Arthur Norman, Alan Mycroft, and Richard O'Keefe for their insights and interest in Prolog. I particularly thank Ian Lewis for his valuable assistance with the preparation of this book, including the contribution of ideas for worksheets and case studies. In particular, Ian provided the ideas and code for the case study on functional programming. Finally, I thank those who read and commented upon the first draft of this book, including Ralph Becket and Ian Lewis. Of course the individuals named here are not responsible for the errors or infelicities that remain.

Swaffham Prior   W.F.C.
April 1997

Table of Contents

CHAPTER ONE
GETTING STARTED

Prolog is the most widely used programming language to have been inspired by logic programming research. There are a number of reasons for the popularity of Prolog as a programming language:

- Powerful symbol manipulation facilities, including unification with logical variables. Programmers can consider logical variables as named 'holes' in data structures. Unification also serves as the parameter passing mechanism, and provides a constructor and selector of data structures. When combined with recursive procedures and a surface syntax for data structures, the symbol manipulation possibilities of Prolog surpass those of other languages.

- Automatic backtracking provides generate-and-test as the basic control flow model. This is more general than the strict uni-directional sequential flow of control in conventional languages. Although generate-and-test is not appropriate for some applications, other control flow models can be programmed to correspond to the demands of a particular application.

- Program clauses and data structures have the same form. This gives a unified model for representing data as programs and programs as data. Other languages such as Lisp also have this feature.

- The procedural interpretation of clauses, together with a back-tracking control structure, provides a convenient way to express and to use nondeterministic procedures. However, the price to pay is the occasional necessity to employ extralogical control features such as fail and cut.

- The relational form of clauses lends the possibility to define 'procedures' that can be used for more than one purpose. It is the responsibility of the programmer to ensure whether a particular procedure completely implements a given relation.

- A Prolog program can be regarded as a relational database that contains rules as well as facts. It is easy to add and remove information from the database, and to pose sophisticated queries.

1.1   Syntax

Everything (programs and data structures) in Prolog is constructed from terms. There are three kinds of terms: constants, variables and compound terms:

A *constant* names an individual. Constants are further divided into *numbers* and *atoms*. Numbers are the usual signed integer and floating-point numbers. Examples of numbers are 17, 17.2, -65, -0.22E+07. There are several ways to write atoms:

(a) An atom may begin with a lower-case letter which may be followed by digits and letters and may include the underscore character. For example, alpha, gross_pay, john_smith.

(b) An atom may also consist of a sequence of *sign characters*, for example, +, **, Λ, =/=.

(c) An atom may be any sequence of characters enclosed in single-quotes, for example, '12Q&A'. Quotes may or may not be necessary, depending on the sequence of characters making up the name. For example, this and 'this' denote the same atom.

A *variable* stands for a term. A variable begins with an upper-case letter or underscore character which may be followed by digits and letters and may include the underscore character. For example, X, Gross_pay, _257. A single underscore character names the *anonymous variable*. An anonymous variable is distinct from any other variable. Its uses will be described later.

A *compound term* names an individual by its parts. A compound term consists of a *functor* and one or more *arguments*. The arguments may be any terms. The arguments are written separated by commas and enclosed in a pair of round brackets. The number of arguments of a compound term is called its *arity*.

For example,

likes(john,mary)

is a compound term with functor likes of arity 2, and arguments john and mary. The term

++(V, inc(a), 128)

has functor ++ of arity 3, with arguments V (which is a variable), inc(a), and 128. The argument inc(a) is itself a compound term with functor inc of arity 1 and argument a.

The taxonomy of terms is illustrated as follows, showing examples in the boxes:

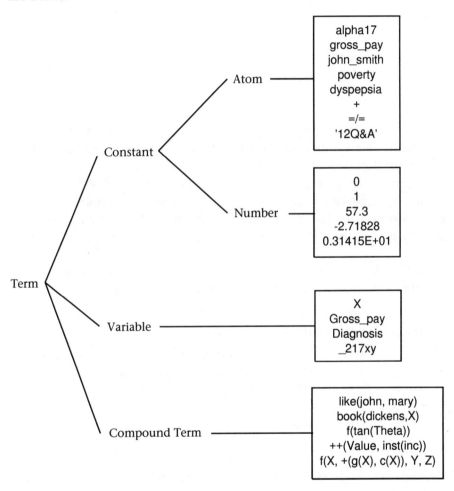

1.1.1 Operator Notation

Any atom may be designated as an operator. This does not change the meaning of the atom. The only purpose of operators is for convenience. Whether an atom is designated as an operator only affects how the term containing the atom is parsed. So, if '+' is declared as an infix operator, the term 3+17 is not the same thing as the integer 20. The plus sign does not automatically mean 'add'. It is simply the functor of a term which could just as well be written +(3,17).

Operators have three properties: position, priority, and associativity. The position of an operator may be prefix, infix, or postfix. Here are some examples:

	Operator Syntax	Equivalent to
Prefix:	-a	-(a)
Infix:	5+17	+(5,17)
Postfix:	N!	!(N)

Once an atom is designated as an operator, the operator syntax shown for the above examples may be used. This is equivalent to a Prolog term which also can be written in the usual way.

Associativity and precedence determine how operators bind to arguments relative to other operators in the term. In Prolog, operators may associate on the right, on the left, or prohibit association. The priority is an integer from 1 to 1200, with lower numbers binding more tightly.

Although we won't be declaring any operators for the moment, it is useful to know the built-in declarations of commonly used operators:

Operator	Class	Priority	Used for
:-	xfx	1200	Separating head and body of a clause
,	xfy	1000	Separating goals in a clause
is	xfx	700	Arithmetic evaluation
+ −	yfx	500	
* /	yfx	400	
−	fy	200	

The class is used to encode position and associativity. The 'f' represents an operator in a term in which 'x' and possibly 'y' represent subterms. The yfx declaration for '+' above means that '+' is a binary (arity 2) operator that associates on the left, so for example the term a+b+c is parsed as (a+b)+c.

Notice that the same atom may have more than one operator declaration, so the hyphen '-' may be used as a binary (arity 2) operator and a unary (arity 1) operator, depending on the context in which it appears in the expression. The ':-' and 'is' operators prohibit association to reduce the risk of syntax errors. In any expression, round brackets may be used to enforce the association of subexpressions in a way that overrides the operator declaration.

1.1.2   Trees

In this book, terms will often be drawn in tree form. Drawing terms this way graphically depicts the syntactic structure of programs and data structures. An *n*-ary compound term is drawn as a node (its functor) having *n* branches (its arguments). Constants and variables appear as the leaves of the tree. For example, the terms

parents(fido, spot, rover)

and

equal(15+X, (0*a)+(2-5))

are depicted as:

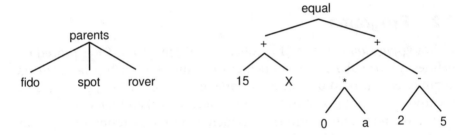

Although the equal term looks like an arithmetic expression, it is important to remember that no arithmetic interpretation is necessarily made. This term is just like any other. Later we shall see how terms that look like arithmetic expressions may be given a special interpretation as arithmetic expressions and be evaluated as such.

Sometimes it is useful to draw trees in a slightly different way. For example, suppose we have a binary (that is, having arity 2) term which is deeply nested on one of the arguments, such as

n(4, n(3, n(2, n(1, n(0, 0)))))

Although the tree shown on the left looks like a tree, the drawing on the right is usually more convenient, because it shows the linear structure of the term and takes up less vertical space on the page:

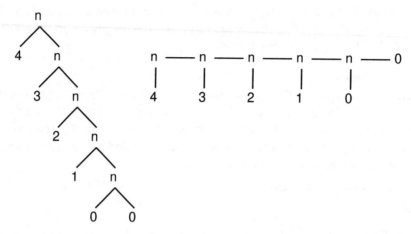

You should be able to see that the two drawings depict equivalent data structures.

1.2 Programs

A Prolog *program* consists of a collection of *procedures*. Each procedure defines a particular *predicate*, being a certain relationship between its arguments. A procedure consists of one or more assertions, or *clauses*. It is convenient to think of two kinds of clauses: *facts* and *rules*.

If T is a term of the form H :- B (where H and B are terms and ':-' is an infix functor), then T is called a rule. The term H is called the *head*, and B is called the *body* of the clause. If the :- sign and the body are missing, then T is called a *fact*. When facts and rules are written down to make a program, each one is terminated by a dot (that is, the 'full stop' or 'period' character).

Here is an example of a procedure drink consisting of three clauses, all facts:

```
drink(beer).
drink(milk).
drink(water).
```

If the body of a rule consists of n terms $G_1, G_2, ..., G_n$ separated by commas, then all the G are called *goals*. In the next example, procedure likes consists of two clauses: one fact and one rule. The rule is defined in terms of goals human and honest. Procedures defining these would need to appear elsewhere in the program:

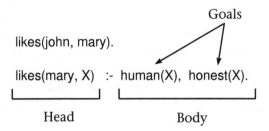

likes(john, mary).

likes(mary, X) :- human(X), honest(X).

Head   Body

Clauses can be given a declarative reading or a procedural reading. For example, the clause

$$H :- G_1, G_2, \ldots, G_n.$$

can be read declaratively as

"That H is provable follows from goals $G_1, G_2, \ldots, G_n$ being provable"

or procedurally as

"In order to execute procedure H, the procedures called by goals $G_1, G_2, \ldots, G_n$ should be executed."

Before turning to the mechanics of program execution, we need to introduce unification.

1.3   Unification

Unification is a basic operation on terms. Two terms *unify* if substitutions can be made for any variables in the terms so that the terms are made identical. If no such substitution exists, then the terms do not unify. Unification is a very powerful technique, and in Prolog, unification is used for passing actual parameters, 'pattern matching', and database access. In the *Programming in Prolog* book, unification is called 'matching', because it is a more descriptive word. This was probably misjudged, because in computer science the word 'matching' is more often used in another sense to mean the less powerful one-way pattern matching such as what the language ML does.

An algorithm for unification proceeds by recursive descent of the two input terms: when attempting to unify two terms, determine whether their corresponding components unify. Ultimately, constants, variables and compund terms will be compared. The rules are as follows:

- *Constants* unify if they are identical. For example, john will unify with john, but john and mary will not unify.

- *Variables* unify with any term, including other variables. When as a result of unification a term has been substituted for a variable, we say that the variable is *instantiated* to the term. For example, the constant alpha will unify with the variable X, and then in all places where the variable X appears in the term, it will be replaced by alpha. If two variables unify with each other, then they *co-refer*: that is, the both refer to the same term. The anonymous variable will unify with any term, and does not co-refer with any term.

- *Compound terms* unify if their functors and all their components unify.

Examples:

1. The compound terms f(X,a(b,c)) and f(d,a(Z,c)) unify, instantiating X to d and Z to b. Look at this tree diagram showing the two terms. The dotted lines depict the instantiations.

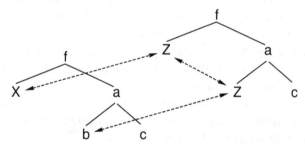

2. The terms f(X,a(b,c)) and f(Z,a(Z,c)) unify, instantiating X to b and Z to b. Look:

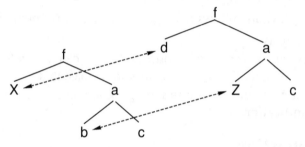

Notice that in the term f(Z, a(Z,c)), that the two Z's already co-refer. Like-named variables in the same term always co-refer.

3. The terms f(c,a(b,c)) and f(Z,a(Z,c)) do not unify. Why not? Because Z cannot be instantiated to both b and c at the same time.

Practice

1. By trying several possible instantiations of variables, confirm the claim made in the previous example, that Z cannot be instantiated to both b and c at the same time.

2. Notice how these terms match:

> g(Z,f(A,17,B),A+B,17) and g(C,f(D,D,E),C,E).

Draw in the arrows between the two terms. To which terms are the variables instantiated? Here are tree diagrams to help:

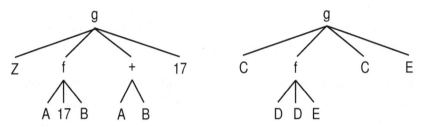

1.4 Execution Model

Given a program consisting of clauses, the way to use the program is to pose *queries* about it. The precise manner in which queries are posed depends on the Prolog system you use, but we shall assume an interactive session, and that a query is prefixed by the sign '?-'. So, given the program

> drink(beer).
> drink(milk).
> drink(water).

the query

> ?- drink(milk).

asks the Prolog system to test whether the query logically follows from the clauses in the program. Prolog searches from the top of the program to the bottom. The next clause it finds could be a fact or a rule.

- When it finds a fact, it tries to unify the query with the fact. If there is a unifier, one solution has been found. If there is no unifier, it tries the next clause in the program.
- If it finds a rule, it tries to unify the query with the head of the rule. If there is a unifier, the subgoals in the body of the clause are treated as that queries which must be satisfied in order for the original query to be satisfied. If the query cannot be unified with the head of the rule, it tries the next clause in the program.

For the above program and query, the query unifies with the second clause, so Prolog answers

> *yes*

(In this book, answers from the Prolog system will appear in italics.)
If the query had been

   ?- drink(2+6).

Prolog would answer

   no

because there is no way that the term drink(2+6) can be derived from the
program. More usefully, if the query is

   ?- drink(X).

we are asking the Prolog system to find a value for X that logically
follows from the clauses in the program. The first solution according to
the above program is

   X = beer

There are more solutions, because there are three possible choices from
the program that unify with drinks(X). Depending on which Prolog
system you are using, there are various ways to ask for the next
solution, and we shall see how to do this later.

What about rules? Suppose our program is about who drinks what:

   drinks(john, water).
   drinks(jeremy, milk).
   drinks(camilla, beer).
   drinks(jeremy, X) :- drinks(john, X).

The first three facts are straightforward: the first argument of each drinks
clause is a person's name, and the second argument is the drink which
is drunk by that person. The last clause, a rule, says that jeremy also
drinks anything that john drinks.

By posing various queries, we can find out who drinks what:

   ?- drinks(camilla, X)

   X = beer

   ?- drinks(X, gin).

   no.

The more interesting query is to find out what jeremy drinks. From the
above program, you should be able to tell that jeremy drinks milk (by
virtue of clause 2), and that he also drinks water (because according to
clause 4, he drinks whatever john drinks, and according to clause 1, john
drinks water). All the possibilities for what jeremy drinks can be depicted
in this 'proof tree':

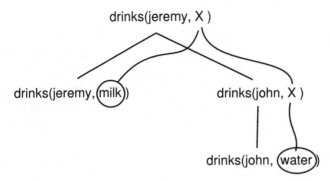

The straight lines show how one goal sets up another goal. The curved lines show the alternative values for X for different solutions.

The general case is of a sequence of queries that must be satisfied. The subgoals in a query are separated by commas. Prolog begins from left to right attempting to satisfy each query. If a subgoal succeeds, Prolog tries the next one on the right. If a subgoal fails, Prolog goes back to the goal on the left to see if there are any more solutions. So, if we wish to test whether some X is human and honest, the query

   ?- human(X), honest(X).

is executed. This picture might help:

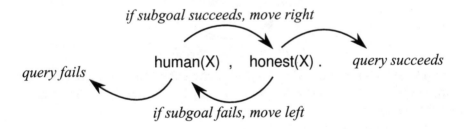

This way of showing how success and failure propagate though a sequence of subgoals works for any number of subgoals in the body of a clause.

Worksheet 1: Party Pairs

We are organising a party. We need to decide whether a pair of people will dance together. The single rule for dancing together is that the pair will consist of a male and a female. We begin the program with some males and females. The predicate male is defined such that the goal male(X) succeeds with the name X of a male. The predicate female is defined such that the goal female(X) succeeds for the name X of a female:

```
male(bertram).
male(percival).

female(lucinda).
female(camilla).
```

Next, the rule for a pair. The predicate pair is defined such that the goal pair(X, Y) succeeds for a pair consisting of a male X and female Y.

```
pair(X, Y) :- male(X), female(Y).
```

In order for pair to succeed, both the male and female goals need to succeed. Recall this pattern:

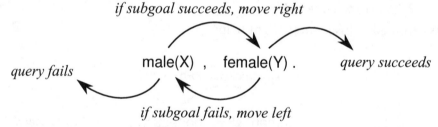

Practice. What happens for the following goals? Indicate what the first answer is (if any), and what the subsequent answers are (if any) on backtracking.

```
?- pair(percival, X).
?- pair(apollo, daphne).
?- pair(camilla, X).
?- pair(X, lucinda).
?- pair(X, X).
?- pair(bertram, lucinda).
?- pair(X, fido).
?- pair(X, Y).
```

You should know that the solution set of the last goal is the Cartesian product of the male and female relations.

Worksheet 2: Drinking Pairs

We are still organising a party. We need to decide whether a pair of people will drink the same drink. The database begins with the predicate drinks, which is defined such that the goal drinks(X, Y) succeeds for person X who drinks drink Y.

    drinks(john, martini).
    drinks(mary, gin).
    drinks(susan, vodka).
    drinks(john, gin).
    drinks(fred, gin).

Next, our rule for a drinking pair. The predicate pair is defined such that the goal pair(X, Y, Z) succeeds for a pair consisting of people X and Y who drink Z:

    pair(X, Y, Z) :- drinks(X, Z), drinks(Y, Z).

Practice. What happens for the following goals? Indicate what the first answer is (if any), and what the subsequent answers are (if any) on backtracking.

    ?- pair(X, john, martini).

    ?- pair(mary, susan, gin).

    ?- pair(john, mary, gin).

    ?- pair(john, john, gin).

    ?- pair(X, Y, gin).

    ?- pair(bertram, lucinda, vodka).

    ?- pair(X, Y, Z).

You will have found that nothing prevents pair from deciding that person X drinks with person X. We wish to put a stop to this unsociable behaviour. The predicate '\==', with a built-in declaration as an infix operator, succeeds if its two arguments are not identical. Another definition of pair might look like this:

    pair(X, Y, Z) :- drinks(X, Z), drinks(Y, Z), X \== Y.

Worksheet 3: Affordable Journeys

We now wish to travel. We are given a geographical map representing counties in Southern England as follows:

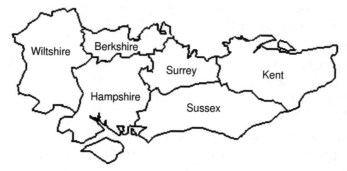

Before somebody writes in to complain about my map, I should just admit that East and West Sussex have been merged, and the Isle of Wight has no label.

A graph can be depicted as the dual of the geographical map, where the arcs represent the binary border relation:

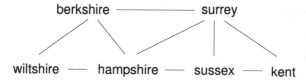

This graph can be represented as the predicate border as follows:

    border(sussex, kent).
    border(sussex, surrey).
    border(surrey, kent).
    border(hampshire, sussex).
    border(hampshire, surrey).
    border(hampshire, berkshire).
    border(berkshire, surrey).
    border(wiltshire, hampshire).
    border(wiltshire, berkshire).

This definition is an incomplete representation as it stands, because in real life we know that borders are symmetric: if Sussex borders Kent, then it is true that Kent borders Sussex. But in the above predicate we have asserted border(sussex, kent), and we have not also said border(kent,sussex). To be able to travel in both directions across a border, we need to make explicit the symmetry of borders. This can be border, we need to make explicit the symmetry of borders. This can be done in either of two ways. The first way is to double the size of the above definition by writing, for each clause above, a corresponding clause with the arguments reversed. So, for example, we would have to augment the above clauses with

```
border(kent, sussex).
border(surrey, sussex).
border(kent, surrey).
    ⋮
```

and so forth. Making symmetry explicit in this way doubles the number of clauses needed, and this is not necessarily a good idea. Another way is to leave border as it is, and define the adjacent predicate, which adds only two clauses:

```
adjacent(X,Y) :- border(X,Y).
adjacent(X,Y) :- border(Y,X).
```

So now, adjacent(kent,sussex) will be satisfied by virtue of the second adjacent clause.

Finally, we define what an affordable journey is: a journey that spans no more than two counties:

```
affordable(X,Y) :- adjacent(X,Z), adjacent(Z,Y).
```

Practice. What happens for the following goals?

```
?- affordable(wiltshire, sussex).
?- affordable(wiltshire, kent).
?- affordable(hampshire, hampshire).
?- affordable(X, kent).
?- affordable(sussex, X).
?- affordable(X, Y).
```

Worksheet 4: Acyclic Directed Graph

The easiest way to represent a directed graph is by using facts to represent the arcs between the nodes of the graph. For example,

a(g, h).
a(g, d).
a(e, d).
a(h, f).
a(e, f).
a(a, e).
a(a, b).
a(b, f).
a(b, c).
a(f, c).

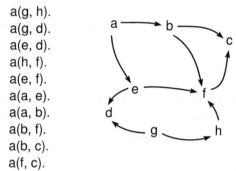

Because we are representing a directed graph, predicate a is interpreted such that the goal a(X,Y) means that there is an arc from X to Y. This does not imply that there is an arc from Y to X. You should know a as the *relation* of the graph.

Do not worry that there is a node named 'a' as well as a relation named 'a'. Prolog keeps these names distinct because it is clear from the syntax that the node a is a constant, and the relation a is the functor of a compound term of arity 2.

The easiest way to search a graph is as follows. We wish to know whether there is a path between two nodes according to the relation given above. The predicate path is defined such that goal path(X,Y) succeeds if there is a path from X to Y:

path(X,X).
path(X,Y) :- a(X, Z), path(Z, Y).

Practice. What happens for each of the following goals? Does back-tracking provide multiple answers? If so, why?

?-path(f, f).
?- path(a, c).
?- path(g, e).
?- path(g, X).
?- path(X, h).

What determines the order in which the graph is searched?

CHAPTER TWO
DATA STRUCTURES

So far the only programs we have looked at are those using constants and variables. Now we shall turn to structured data. As we saw before, structured data is represented by compound terms. One useful elementary data structure is the *list*. A list is an arbitrarily long finite sequence of terms called *elements* of the list. Prolog has a source syntax for lists, in which the elements of the list are separated by commas and enclosed in square brackets. The following are examples of lists written in the source syntax:

```
[a, b, c]
[a+17, f(X-32, Y+17)]]
[]
[[the, cat], sat]
[[the, [rabbit]], [was, pulled], [from, [the, [hat]]]]
```

If a list contains *n* elements, we say that the list is 'of length *n*'. The theory of lists is very simple.

- The list of length 0 is called the *null list*. The null list is also sometimes called *nil* or the *nil list* or the *empty list*. In Prolog, the null list is written [], that is, a pair of square brackets with nothing in them.

- The list of length *n* is represented by the compound term .(*x*,*y*), where the functor is '.' of arity 2, *x* is an element of the list, and *y* is a list of length *n*–1. The functor is the dot (the 'full stop' or 'period') character. The element *x* is called the *head* of the list, and the list *y* is called the *tail* of the list.

Normally we use the source syntax described above. However, it is useful to know the dot notation, which is just the ordinary compound term notation. Here are some examples of dot notation:

[]
.(a,[])
.(a, .(b,[]))
.(a, .(b, .(c, .(d, .(e, [])))))
.(a,b)
.(a,X)
.(.(a, .(b,[])), .(c,[]))

Notice that, according to the above definition, the last three examples are not proper lists. In the expression .(a,b), there is the constant b where [] would have to be if it were a list. In the expression .(a,X), there is a variable, which, if correctly instantiated, would rectify the example into a list. In the final example, although elements of the example are lists, the top-level structure is not a list.

Practice. Match up the above lists with their equivalent tree drawings shown here:

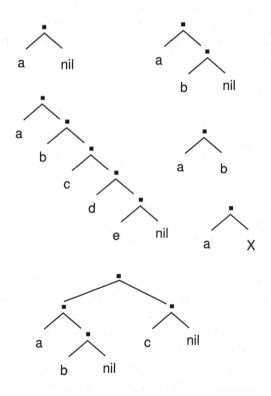

2.1   Square Bracket Notation

Using the source syntax,

- The null list is written [].
- The list consisting of n elements $t_1, t_2, \ldots, t_n$ is written $[t_1, t_2, \ldots, t_n]$.

There is a correspondence between the ordinary compound term notation using dots, and the square bracket notation. Notice how the vertical bar is used:

- $.(x, y)$ is written $[\,x \mid y\,]$
- $[\,x \mid [\,]\,]$ is written $[\,x\,]$

For example, the term .(a, .(b, .(c,Y))) is written [a, b, c | Y]. If Y becomes instantiated to [], then the example is a list, and can be written

   [a, b, c | []]

or simply [a, b, c]. The vertical bar can be mistaken for a capital letter 'l' or the digit '1', so take care when reading and writing programs.

Practice. Identify the head and tail (if any) of these lists:

   [a, b, c]
   [a]
   []
   [[the, cat], sat]
   [[the, [rabbit]], [was pulled], [from, [the, [hat]]]]

Because lists are just terms, they may be unified with other terms. Because the length of a list corresponds with the depth of the term, unification has an effect over the entire list.

Practice. For each pair of lists given below, determine whether they unify, and if so, give the terms to which the variables are instantiated.

   [X, Y, Z]   [john, likes, fish]
   [cat]   [X | Y]
   [X, Y | Z]   [mary, likes, wine]
   [[the ,Y] | Z]   [[X, answer], [is, here]]
   [X, Y, X]   [a, Z, Z]
   [[X], [Y], [X]]   [[a], [Z], [Z]]

Worksheet 5: Member

The easiest thing to do with a list is to determine whether a given term is an element of the list. We shall define predicate member, such that given a term X and a list L, the goal member(X, L) succeeds if X is one of the elements of L. This is written in the recursive style, requiring a base case and a recursive case. The base case shows that X is a member of the list if X is the first element (or the 'head') of the list. We can test this by unifying X with the head of the list. The recursive case shows that X is a member of the list if X is a member of the tail of the list.

```
member(X, [X|T]).
member(X, [H|T]) :- member(X,T).
```

If X is not a member of the list, eventually the subgoal member(X, []) will be attempted, and this subgoal fails because there is no way to unify it with either of the clauses given above. The failure will be propagated back up the recursion to fail the original goal.

Practice. In the first clause above, what is T for? In the second clause, what is H for? What do the following goals do (what is the first answer if any, and then what are subsequent answers if any on backtracking)?

```
?- member(john, [paul, john]).

?- member(X, [paul, john]).

?- member(joe, [marx, darwin, freud])

?- member(foo, X).
```

Suppose the following predicate has been defined:

```
mystery(X, A, B) :- member(X, A), member(X, B).
```

What do the following goals do?

```
?- mystery(a, [b,c,a] , [p,a,l]).

?- mystery(b, [b,l,u,e], [y,e,l,l,o,w]).

?  mystery(X, [r,a,p,i,d], [a,c,t,i,o,n]).

?- mystery(X, [w,a,l,n,u,t], [c,h,e,r,r,y]).
```

Variables that appear only once in a clause do not co-refer with any other variable, so may be written as anonymous variables. The first clause of member may be written as

```
member(X, [X|_]).
```

How may an anonymous variable be written in the second clause of member?

2.2 Arithmetic

Prolog provides a built-in predicate for the purpose of evaluating terms according to the rules of arithmetic. This predicate is called 'is', and it can be written as an infix operator. The predicate is is defined such that the goal X is Y succeeds if Y is a term that when evaluated according to the rules of arithmetic, yields an integer that unifies with X. For example,

> ?- X is 2+2*2.
>
> *X = 6*
>
> ?- 10 is (2*0)+2«4.
>
> *no*

Suppose we define a predicate coeff, such that goal coeff(A, X, B, Y) succeeds if Y is the result of calculating A*X+B:

> coeff(A,X,B,Y) :- Y is A*X+B.

Note the following goals:

> ?- coeff(2, 2, 2, 6).
>
> *yes*
>
> ?- coeff(1+7, 2*2, 4, Y).
>
> *Y = 36*

Variables in the second argument of is may be instantiated to integers or terms (which are recursively evaluated), but must be instantiated. The terms of the second argument of is may be constructed from a variety of structures, which may be written as infix (if binary) or prefix (if unary). Consult your reference manual for details. In particular, Prolog provides a built-in predicate for the purpose of comparing two arithmetic expressions for equality. The predicate =\=, which can be written as an infix operator, is defined such that the goal X =\= Y succeeds if X and Y do not evaluate to the same number. Ensure you know the difference between =\= and \==. Finally, the other usual arithmetic comparisons are available, where X and Y need to be instantiated to terms that evaluate as arithmetic expressions:

X =:= Y	equal
X > Y	greater than
X >= Y	greater than or equal to
X < Y	less than
X =< Y	less than or equal to

Worksheet 6: Length of a List

We want to find out how many elements are in a list. We say that a list has length *n* if there are *n* elements in the list. Given a list L and an integer N, the goal length(L, N) succeeds if the length of the list L is N. You can write this program in two ways. Both ways are recursive: they require a base case and a general recursive case.

The first way is as follows. The base case says that the length of the null list is 0. The recursive case says the length of any non-nil list is the length of its tail plus 1.

```
length([], 0)
length([H|T], N) :- length(T, Nt),  N is Nt + 1.
```

The next way to write this uses the same recursive principle, but the answer is accumulated in a variable used for this purpose. The accumulator would be initialised to 0 by the caller of length. First, the calling routine:

```
length(L, N) :- accumulate(L, 0, N).
```

The auxiliary predicate accumulate is defined such that the goal accumulate(L, M, N) succeeds if the length of list L is M+N. In the situation here, where the action of the accumulator is to add for each step, the accumulator M should be initialised to the identity element for addition, namely 0, as shown above.

The program for accumulate has two clauses. First, for the null list, the length of the list will be whatever has been accumulated so far. Second, we add 1 to the accumulated amount given, and recur on the tail of the list.

```
accumulate([], A, A).
accumulate([H|T], A, N) :- A1 is A + 1, accumulate(T, A1, N).
```

Practice. What is H for? In the first clause of accumulate, why must we never replace the A variables by anonymous variables? What do each of the following goals do (use your favourite definition of length)?

```
?- length([apple,pear], N).
?- length(L, 3).
?- length([alpha], 2).
```

The length procedure can be modified to give a sum procedure, defined such that the goal sum(L, N) succeeds if L is a list of integers and N is their sum. Modify length accordingly.

Worksheet 7: Inner Product

A list of n integers can be used to represent an n-vector. The inner product (or dot product) of two vectors $\underline{a}$ and $\underline{b}$ is defined as

$$\underline{a} \cdot \underline{b} = \sum_{i=1}^{n} a_i \cdot b_i .$$

That is, the inner product is the sum of the component-by-component products of the two vectors. The inner product is only defined for two vectors of the same length. Define the predicate inner, such that the goal inner(V1, V2, P) succeeds for the pair of lists V1 and V2 and their inner product P.

Note there are two ways to do this, depending on when the recursive call takes place. The preferable program is a tail-recursive one that uses the idea of an accumulator for keeping the 'partial product so far'. Here is the naive non-accumulating version first:

```
inner([], [], 0).
inner([A|As], [B|Bs], N) :- inner(As, Bs, Ns), N is Ns + (A * B).
```

Now the preferred version, the tail-recursive one, which uses an accumulator (the third argument), initialised to 0:

```
inner(A, B, N) :- dotaux(A, B, 0, N).

dotaux([], [], V, V).
dotaux([A|As], [B|Bs], N, Z) :- N1 is N + (A * B), dotaux(As, Bs, N1, Z).
```

You should be able to see the similarity between this and the program for accumulating the length of a list.

Practice. What happens if the lengths of the two list vectors are different?

Worksheet 8: Maximum of a List

We are given a list of numbers, and we wish to find out which one of the numbers is numerically the largest. This can be done by means of an accumulator representing the 'largest number found so far'. Given a list L and an accumulator A, the goal max(L, A, M) succeeds if M is the largest element of the list greater than A. The goal must initialise the accumulator to a sensible value.

The program contains a base case and two recursive cases. The base case is used when the input list is nil, so the result must be the largest integer to have been found thus far (the accumulator). The second case is used when the next element of the list is greater than the accumulator. We simply recur on the tail of the input list, with the new value of the accumulator. Otherwise, the third case is used, to recur on the tail of the list with the same accumulator as before.

```
max([], A, A).
max([H|T], A, M) :- H > A, max(T, H, M).
max([H|T], A, M) :- H <= A, max(T, A, M).
```

Initialisation of the accumulator argument can be hidden by defining an interface procedure. One possibility is to initialise the accumulator to the smallest number you can think of, for example:

```
maximum(L, M) :- max(L, -100000, M).
```

This method is not recommended, because it is not wise to rely on arbitrary quantities, and one day you might be able to think of another, smaller number. One possibility is to define a version of maximum that takes the initial value of the accumulator from the first element of the input list.

Practice

1. Define a version of maximum that initialises the accumulator from the first element of the input list.

2. What do each of the following goals do?

   ```
   ?- max([3,1,4,1,5,8,2,6], 0, N).
   ?- max([2,4,7,7,7,2,1,6], 5, N).
   ```

3. Define the procedure min, which finds the minimum of a list. How should the accumulator be initialised? Define the procedure minmax, which finds both the minimum and maximum values in a list. A typical subgoal would appear as

   ```
   ..., minmax(L, MinVal, MaxVal), ... .
   ```

Worksheet 9: Searching a Cyclic Graph

Here we have a similar graph to the one on Worksheet 4 (page 16), but we have added an arc between d and a:

a(g, h).
a(d, a).
a(g, d).
a(e, d).
a(h, f).
a(e, f).
a(a, e).
a(a, b).
a(b, f).
a(b, c).
a(f, c).

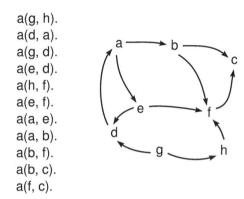

If we use the previous path program on this relation, the goal

   ?- path(a, b).

will cause the program on Worksheet 4 to loop. You should take a moment to satisfy yourself that the program will in fact loop (this is given as a practice session below).

   A way to prevent loops is to keep a 'trail' of the nodes we have visited so far. We now visit only legal nodes. A node is legal if it is not on the trail. The trail can be represented as an extra argument of predicate path, defined such that the goal path(X ,Y ,T) succeeds if there is a legal path from node X to node Y, without passing though any nodes that are in list T.

   path(X, X, T)
   path(X, Y, T) :- a(X, Z), legal(Z, T), path(Z, Y, [Z|T]).
   legal(Z, []).
   legal(Z, [H|T]) :- Z \== H, legal(Z, T).

Notice that predicate legal is like the negation of predicate member. Also, note that the trail is actually a kind of accumulator.

Practice. Why will the program in Worksheet 4 loop when given the above database? What do the following goals do given the new program? Remember backtracking.

   ?- path(g, c, []).
   ?- path(g, c, [f]).
   ?- path(a, X, [f,d]).

CHAPTER THREE
MAPPING

In the previous chapters we have been concerned with *valuations*. If we consider a goal as an implementation of a box to which we give an input and obtain an output, valuations are kinds of goals (or boxes) that give a point value.

$$[a, b, c] \longrightarrow \boxed{} \longrightarrow b$$

For example, the *length* of a list, the *maximum element* of a list, a *node* that is reachable from another node in a graph – all these we call point values, and a predicate such as member is called a valuation:

Of course, because Prolog is relational, it is possible for predicate such as member to construct an 'input' list given one of its members, like this:

$$b \longrightarrow$$
$$\text{member}(\quad , \quad) \longrightarrow [b \mid \_]$$

In any discussion of valuations we cannot exclude this possibility, nor also the possibility that member may simply succeed (or fail) with arguments as given, without necessarily 'producing' anything we did not already know, as depicted here:

$$\longrightarrow \text{member}([a,b,c], \ b) \longrightarrow$$

In this chapter we shall introduce *mappings*. A mapping is a relation between two data structures x and y, where each component of y is related to *x* by some valuation on each component of *x*. Mapping is a powerful and general idea from which programs can be composed.

For example, suppose we are given an input list, and we wish to produce an output list whose elements are transformations of corresponding elements of the input list. This is called *mapping* the input list to the output list. We distinguish between *full mapping*, which maps each element of the input onto an element of the output, and *partial mapping*, which maps only some of the input elements onto output elements. To illustrate full and partial maps on lists, here is a full map which maps each element of a list to its double:

$$[1, 2, 3, 4] \longrightarrow [2, 4, 6, 8]$$

and here is a partial map in which the output contains only the positive even elements of the input:

$$[57, -2, 34, -21] \longrightarrow [34]$$

There are also multiple maps, in which an input list is mapped into several outputs. Some multiple maps are *disjoint*, meaning that the output lists are disjoint. To illustrate, here is a multiple disjoint map that splits a list into its non-negative and negative elements:

$$[57, -2, 34, -21] \begin{cases} [57, 34] \\ [-2, -21] \end{cases}$$

Some maps have *state*, meaning that state variables help to determine the ouput lists. Maps with state can be *sequential*, meaning that for ordered data structures, the state variable determining a particular output value depends only on input values previous in the sequence. Run-length encoding is an illustration of a sequential map:

$$[a, a, f, 3, 3, 3, w, f, f, f, f, 3, 3] \longrightarrow [2^*a, 1^*f, 3^*3, 1^*w, 4^*f, 2^*3]$$

Here the output list is an encoding of the input list that says, "two a's, one f, three 3's, one w, four f's, and two 3's." It is possible to reconstruct the input list given the information in the output list, so this mapping does not lose information.

Some maps with state can be *scattered*, meaning that the output value can depend on any of the input values. Finding a frequency distribution is an example of a scattered map, because the frequency distribution does not preserve information about location in the input list:

$$[a, a, f, 3, 3, 3, w, f, f, f, f, 3, 3] \longrightarrow [2^*a, 5^*f, 5^*3, 1^*w]$$

Here the output list is an encoding of the input list that says, "two a's, five f's, five 3's, and one w." It is not possible to reconstruct the input list given the frequency distribution, because locational information is lost.

Of course, maps are not restricted to lists, but may concern any compound data structure. In the worksheets we shall be seeing mapping applied not only to lists but to trees.

It is customary in functional and logic programming to define abstractions of mappings by using higher-order functions. This can be a useful technique, because programs can be simplified where common patterns of recursion might otherwise be used. However, we shall not be doing this in the worksheets because our aim here is to expose interesting patterns of computation, not to encapsulate them. Instead, one of the case studies will consider higher-order programming, and there we shall see ways in which mapping can be abstracted.

Worksheet 10: Full Maps

We shall first consider full mapping. A predicate that maps a list of integers onto their squares is as follows. Predicate sqlist is defined such that the goal sqlist(X,Y) succeeds if Y is a list of the squares of the integers in X.

```
sqlist([], []).
sqlist([X|T], [Y|L]) :- Y is X * X, sqlist(T, L).
```

Using mapping we are creating a new list where each member of the new list is a transformed version of the corresponding element in the original list.

The pattern is always the same. A base case is needed to map the null list to the null list. A recursive case is needed to match the input head and tail, transform the input head to the output head, and recur on the input tail to obtain the output tail.

Here is another program, given by way of exercise in using compound terms, that maps each integer in the input list to a compound term of the form s(X,Y), where Y is the square of X:

```
sqterm([], []).
sqterm([X|T], [s(X,Y)|L]) :- Y is X * X, sqterm(T, L).
```

The general scheme for a full map is as follows:

```
fullmap([], []).
fullmap([X|T], [Y|L]) :- transform(X, Y), fullmap(T, L).
```

Practice. Consider the following program:

```
envelope([], []).
envelope([X|T], [container(X)|L]) :- envelope(T, L).
```

What does the goal envelope([apple, peach, cat, 37, john], X) do?

Using a scheme like fullmap, give a suitable definition that encodes words in a limited vocabulary to words in a fictitious language. For example, encoding words as arbitrary integers, the following goal might execute as follows:

```
?- fullmap([the, cat, sits, on, the, mat], X].
    X = [17, 23, 46, 9, 17, 2].
```

Worksheet 11: Multiple Choices

With mapping it is necessary to account for each element of the input list, or else the goal may fail. For example, suppose we wish to map all the integers in the list onto their squares, and if there are any non-integers in the list, they will be mapped onto themselves. For example,

?- squint([1, 3, w, 5, goat], X).

X = [1, 9, w, 25, goat].

Here is an incomplete program that attempts to do this:

```
squint([], []).
squint([X|T],[Y|L]) :- integer(X), Y is X * X, squint(T, L).
```

Although it uses the built-in predicate integer to test whether the next element of the list is an integer, the integer goal will fail if the element is not an integer, causing the original squint query to fail. The problem is that another clause is needed to map the non-integers to the output if the integer goal fails. Here is a program to do this

```
squint([], []).
squint([X|T],[Y|L]) :- integer(X), Y is X * X, squint(T, L).
squint([X|T], [X|L]) :- squint(T, L).
```

If the integer goal fails, the third clause will ensure that the non-integers element is mapped to the output.

This program can demonstrate the reason why it is important to know what will happen when a program backtracks. The problem is that the second and third clauses will both match an arbitrary input element. Under backtracking, integer goals that had previously succeeded will fail, causing the third clause to be chosen. Thus, an entirely legitimate alternative answer for a squint query would be one in which the output list is a copy of the input list. This behaviour runs counter to our expectations of how the program should work. Ideally, one would like to be able to commit to the first solution: that is, if integer succeeds, then eliminate any alternatives from consideration: fail instead of backtracking to an alternative clause. In the next chapter we shall see how to specify this.

Practice. Find all solutions to the query

?- squint([1, 3, w, 5, goat], X).

and determine which clause choices were made to give each solution.

Worksheet 12: Partial Maps

We are given an input list, and we wish to partially map it to an output list. For example, the input might be a list of integers, and the output might be a list of only the even integers in the input:

```
evens([], []).
evens([X|T], [X|L]) :- 0 is X mod 2, evens(T, L).
evens([X|T], L) :- 1 is X mod 2, evens(T, L).
```

The mod functor is written as an infix operator. When evaluated as an arithmetic expression on the right-hand side of an 'is', it returns the remainder of the integer division of its arguments. It is used here to determine whether an integer is odd or even. Here is an example run:

```
?- evens([1, 2, 3, 4, 5, 6], Q).

    Q = [2, 4, 6].
```

Using partial mapping we are transforming each member of a list that satisfies some conditions.

The pattern is always the same. A base case is needed to map the null list to null list. A first recursive case is needed to transform the input head to the output head provided it meets the conditions. A second recursive case is needed if the first case fails.

Other examples of partial maps were seen previously. In particular, member, length, and max are special partial maps that can be called *valuations* because they map a list into a single point value.

Practice. Write a program that 'censors' an input list, by making a new list in which certain prohibited words do not appear. To do this, define a predicate prohibit such that the goal prohibit(X) succeeds if X is a cen-sored word. For example:

```
prohibit(bother).
prohibit(blast).
prohibit(drat).
prohibit(fiddlestick).
```

Define the partial map censor such that the goal censor(X,Y) maps the input list of words onto the output list of words in which no prohibited words appear.

Worksheet 13: Removing Duplicates

A set is an unordered collection of unique elements. By contrast, a list is an ordered collection of elements that may contain duplicates. We say a list is ordered because each element in a list is in a particular place. By 'ordered' we don't here mean whether the elements are in numerical or alphabetical order, but that they are 'ordered' in a certain sequence.

Sometimes it is useful to deal with lists that are guaranteed not to contain duplicates. The problem of removing the duplicate elements of a list can be posed as a mapping problem. The goal setify(X, Y) maps input list X to output Y such that Y contains only the members of X without any duplicates:

```
setify([], []).
setify([X|T], L) :- member(X, T), setify(T, L).
setify([X|T], [X|L]) :- setify(T, L).
```

The first clause checks for the null list. The second clause checks whether the next member of the input list is an element of the rest of the input list. If it is an element, there is no need to include it on the output list (because it will be included later), and the process recurs. The third clause assumes the membership test fails, and so maps the input element to the output element.

Of course, what this program does is not to construct a set, but to construct a list containing unique elements. Such a list can be consider-ed an ordered presentation of the elements of a set.

Practice. The setify procedure is only designed to work when re-moving the duplicates from an input list. Explain why

```
?- setify([a,a,b,c,b], X).
```

succeeds, and

```
?- setify([a,a,b,c,b], [a,c,b]).
```

succeeds, but

```
?- setify([a,a,b,c,b], [a,b,c]).
```

does not succeed.

You should be aware of what happens if setify goals are backtracked. This is an example of where an incorrect answer will be given on solutions subsequent to the first one, and where it would be useful to know how to commit to the first solution. This will be introduced in the next chapter.

Worksheet 14: Partial Maps with a Parameter

A previous worksheet (page 25) showed how to prevent loops by keeping a trail of the nodes visited so far. Here is another way to think about the problem. Because we are allowed to visit each node once only, we can give as one of the arguments to path a complete list of all the nodes in the graph. Then, as a node is visited, it is struck off the list, and the reduced list is given to the recursive call. If there is no element to strike off, then the node is not to be visited. Reducing a list in this way can be posed as a partial mapping.

First we can define the partial map reduce, such that the goal reduce(L, X, M) succeeds for input list L, term X, and output list M. List M contains the elements of L, except for the first occurrence of X. Thus, X is a *parameter* of the partial map which controls which element will be left out. What is special about this definition is that we require reduce to fail if X is not present in the input. Thus, this is not only a partial map, but it is not necessarily fully defined depending on the value of the parameter. A reduce goal fails if there is no 'first occurrence' of X.

    reduce([X|T], X, T).
    reduce([H|T], X, [H|L]) :- reduce(T, X, L).

The first clause checks whether the next element of the input unifies with the parameter. If so, the element is not included in the output list. The second clause assumes that the unification test fails, so maps the input to the output. In both clauses, there is a recursion to deal with the rest of the list. The important feature for the path-finding application is that if the parameter is not found in the input list, the goal will fail.

We can use this for searching as follows. The goal path(X,Y,L) succeeds when there is a path from X to Y consisting of nodes drawn only from the list L:

    path(X, X, L).
    path(X, Y, L) :- a(X, Z), reduce(L, Z, L1), path(Z, Y, L1).

For example, using the arc relation on page 25,

    ?- path(a,b, [a,b,c,d,e,f,g,h]).

    yes

Practice. It is always important to check what happens when goals are backtracked. This is particularly important before we have discussed how to specify commitment, because we are assuming that only the first answer is correct. What happens when reduce is backtracked?

Worksheet 15: Multiple Disjoint Partial Maps

We wish to separate sheep from goats. We define the predicate herd, such that the goal herd(L,S,G) succeeds if S is a list of all the sheep in L, and G is a list of all the goats in L.

```
herd([], [], []).
herd([sheep|T], [sheep|S]), G) :- herd(T,S,G).
herd([goat|T],S,[goat|G]):- herd(T,S,G).
```

Practice. What do the following goals do?

?- herd([sheep, goat, goat, sheep, goat], X, Y).

?- herd([goat, sheep, stone, goat, tree], X, Y).

?- herd(X, [sheep, sheep], [goat, goat]).

Now consider the case when one of the elements of the list is something other than a sheep or a goat. Such goals fail when the above clauses are used. Instead of failing, we would like herd to simply pass over the element, continuing with the remainder of the list. Adding this clause to the end of the above program will accomplish this task:

```
herd([X|T], S, G) :- herd(T, S, G).
```

Now suppose that instead of discarding all of the non-sheep and non-goat elements of the input list, we wish to place them into a list also. We can define the predicate herd such that the goal herd(L,S,G,Z) succeeds if S is a list of all the sheep in L; G is a list of all the goats in L; and Z is a list of anything else in L. The program for this takes four clauses. What are they?

Write a program that splits a list containing an even number of elements into two lists, being the alternate elements of the list. For example,

?- alternate([1, 2, 3, 4, 5, 6], X, Y).

X = [1,3,5]; Y = [2,4,6]

?- alternate([a,b,c,d,e,f], X, Y).

X = [a,c,e]; Y = [b,d,f]

This uses the same idea as separating sheep and goats – the multiple disjoint partial map – but is useful in applications such as the Discrete Fourier Transform, which will be dealt with in a case study.

Worksheet 16: Multiple Disjoint Partial Maps

An *n*×*m* matrix (having *n* rows and *m* columns) can be represented as a list having *n* elements, where each element is an *m*-element list. *Transposition* of a matrix is an operation that interchanges the rows and columns of a matrix, so for example the matrix

[[1, 2, 3],   [[1, 4, 7],
  [4, 5, 6],   transposes to   [2, 5, 8],
  [7, 8, 9]]   [3, 6, 9]]

We can define the predicate transpose in the following way. First we can define the two partial maps firstcol and nextcols, followed by the full map transpose. Goal firstcol(M,C) succeeds for matrix M that has list C as its first column. Goal nextcols(M, N) succeeds for matrix M, such that matrix N contains all the columns of M except for the first column. Goal transpose(M, T) succeeds for matrix M and its transpose T.

    firstcol([], []).
    firstcol([[H|T]|R], [H|Hs]) :- firstcol(R, Hs).

    nextcols([], []).
    nextcols([[H|T]|R], [T|Ts]) :- nextcols(R, Ts).

    transpose([[]|_], []).
    transpose(R, [H|C]) :- firstcol(R, H), nextcols(R, T), transpose(T, C).

Note that the first clause of transpose matches the matrix with empty columns.

Practice. This program is inefficient because it traverses the input matrix twice for each call to transpose. It be improved by defining a multiple disjoint map instead of the two partial maps firstcol and nextcols. Suppose we are given a new second clause for transpose that uses a goal chopcol(R, H, L), where R is a matrix, H is a list being the first column of R, and T is a matrix being the remaining columns of R:

    transpose(R, [H|C]) :- chopcol(R, H, T), transpose(T, C).

Do you see the analogy with the head and tail of a list? Define the predicate chopcol using a multiple disjoint map. Only one traversal of the input list is required, so the following is not an acceptable solution:

    chopcol(R, H, T) :- firstcol(R, H), nextcols(R, T).

Worksheet 17: Full Maps with State

Sometimes we need to compute a full map for which the result depends on the state of the computation. For example, suppose we wish to map a list of integers onto a cumulative list of their sums. For example, the list [1, 3, 2, 5, 4] maps onto the cumulative list [1, 4, 6, 11, 15]. The predicate mapsum is defined such that the goal mapsum(A, B) maps the input list A onto the output list B as described above. To do this, we make use of an auxiliary predicate ms. The goal ms(A, N, B) uses the argument N as an accumulator, initialised to 0.

```
ms([], _, []).
ms([H|T], N, [C|L]) :- C is H + N, ms(T, C, L).

mapsum(A,E) :- ms(A,0,B).
```

Using a full map with state, we are transforming each member of an input list. Each element of the output list depends not only on the corresponding element of the input list, but also on the state of the computation represented by the accumulator argument.

The pattern is always the same. A base case is needed to map the null list to the null list. A recursive case is needed to match the input head and tail, transform the input head to the output head, update the state, and recur on the input tail, new state, and output tail. In the example shown above, the output head and the state are the same, but this is only coincidental.

Practice. Suppose we wish to map a list of elements onto a list of 2-ary structures having functor n, such that the first argument of the structure is the corresponding element of the input list, and the second argument is the integer i if the corresponding element of the input list is the ith member of the input list. For example, the input list

[cabbage, beet, carrot, bean, radish, beet]

maps onto the 'indexed set':

[n(cabbage,1), n(beet,2), n(carrot,3), n(bean,4), n(radish,5), n(beet,6)].

Define the predicate enum(A, B) that maps the input list A onto the indexed set B in the manner described above.

Worksheet 18:   Sequential Maps with State

Sometimes we need to compute a partial map in which the result depends on the state of the computation. We distinguish two types of partial maps: *sequential* and *scattered*. In a sequential partial map, the state is derived from a contiguous sequence of elements in the input list. In the scattered partial map, there is no restriction on the origin of the state. We shall first consider an example of a sequential partial map. Suppose we wish to map a list of constants onto a *run-length encoded* list in which a sequential run of n identical constants c is mapped onto the element $n*c$. For example,

[12, 2, 2, w, 3, 3, s, s, s] maps onto [1*12, 2*2, 1*w, 2*3, 3*s]

Note we are using the 2-ary functor '*' as an infixed operator to denote a multiple: the term X*Y denotes a run of X consecutive Y's. To run-encode a list, we need two extra state variables: one variable to stand for the constant we are currently looking at, and another variable, a counter, to stand for the number of times the current constant has been encountered in the current run. The predicate runcode is defined such that for goal runcode(L, C , N, X), L is the input list, C is the current constant, N is the current run length, and X is the output list.

runcode([], C, N, [N*C]).
runcode([H|T], H, N, Z) :- N1 is N+1, runcode(T, H, N1, Z).
runcode([H|T], C, N, [N*C|Z]) :- H \== C, runcode(T, H, 1, Z).

The first clause checks for the null list, and writes the final result obtained from the state variables. The second clause handles the case where the next element of the list, H, is the same as the current constant. In this case, we recur on the tail of the input, incrementing the counter and keeping the same constant. The final clause handles the case where the second clause fails: when the next element of the input is different from the current constant. In this case, an output term is constructed because we are finished with the current run, and we recur on the tail, initialising the counter to 1 because we have already encountered the first element of a run. The initial goal of runcode is interesting. Using the example in the first paragraph,

?- runcode([12,2,2,w,3,3,s,s,s], C, 0, X).

Practice. Why have we (a) initialised C to an uninstantiated variable, and (b) initialised the counter to 0? Add a clause to runcode which skips over any 'noise' in the input sequence, represented as the constant noise.

Worksheet 19: Scattered Maps with State

We are given a parts list, which is a list of 2-ary 'quantity' structures having functor q. The quantity structure q(N, P) stands for 'a quantity of N parts of type P'. For example, the parts list

   [q(5, table), q(15, chair), q(57, apple)]

is a representation of five tables, fifteen chairs, and fifty-seven apples. Given a parts list possibly containing duplicate parts, we wish to map this onto a parts list containing no duplicates, with the quantities of all like parts summed. Such a list we say is in *collected normal form*. For example, the parts list

   [q(17, duck), q(15, goose). q(41, quail), q(12, goose), q(37, quail)]

is mapped to the list

   [q(17, duck), q(27, goose), q(78, quail)]

which is in collected normal form.

   The predicate coll is defined such that the goal coll(L,M) is a mapping from L to M in which M is in collected normal form:

   coll([], [])
   coll([q(N,X)|R], [q(T,X)|R2]) :- collz(X, N, R,Q, T), coll(Q, R2)

   collz(_, N, [], [], N).
   collz(X ,N, [q(Num,X)|R], Q, T) :- M is N + Num, collz(X ,M, R, Q, T)
   collz(X, N, [Q|R], [Q|Qs], T) :- collz(X, N, R, Qs, T).

Practice. Here is an alternative definition which might be simpler but is not tail-recursive. Arrive at an understanding of both this definition and the one above:

   collect([], [])
   collect([q(N,X) | R], [q(T,X) | R3]) :-
                     collect(R, R2),
                     extract(q(M,X), R2, R3),
                     T is M + N.

   extract(q(0, _), [], []).
   extract(H, [H | T], T).
   extract(X, [Y| T], [Y | T1]) :- X \== Y, extract(X, T, T1).

CHAPTER FOUR
CHOICE AND COMMITMENT

4.1   The 'Cut'

Prolog makes available a special built-in predicate spelled '!', and pronounced 'cut'. The purpose of this predicate is to give control over the backtracking control flow of the executing program. When called, the cut always succeeds, but has the side-effect of removing any alternative choices in effect at the time. It follows that if 'cut' is called when there is only one possible solution, then the 'cut' has no effect. Cut has several uses:

1. To change a non-deterministic predicate into a deterministic (functional) one. For example, we wish to check whether X is a member of a list L. If it is a member, we wish to discard the alternative choices. This is done by a deterministic membercheck predicate, which might be more efficient than the usual member, but cannot be used to generate multiple solutions.

   ```
   membercheck(X, [X|_]) :- !.
   membercheck(X, [_|L]) :- membercheck(X, L).


   ?- membercheck(X, [a, b, c]).

   X = a ;

   no.
   ```

2. To specify the exclusion of some cases by 'committing' to the current choice. For example, the goal max(X,Y,Z) instantiates Z to the greater of X and Y:

   ```
   max(X, Y, X) :- X >= Y.
   max(X, Y, Y) :- X < Y.
   ```

A version using cut might look like:

```
max(X, Y, X) :- X >= Y, !.
max(X, Y, Y).
```

If max is called with X >=Y, the first clause will succeed, and the cut will assure that the second clause (the alternative choice) is never made. The advantage is that Prolog can disregard the second clause as an alternative backtracking choice.

One consequence of the max program being written using a cut is that the test does not have to be made twice if X<Y. The disadvantage is that each rule does not now stand on its own as a logically correct statement about the predicate. This can be considered an unwise practice. To see why, try

```
?- max(10, 0, 0).
```

Therefore, a sound practice is to insert a cut in order to commit to the current clause choice, and also ensure as far as practically possible that clauses are written so as to stand independently as a correct statement about the predicate. Thus, max can be written as the following without reproach:

```
max(X, Y, X) :- X >= Y, !.
max(X, Y, Y) :- X < Y.
```

This issue is further discussed below.

In general, consider two clauses of predicate H of the form:

$$H_1 :- B_1, B_2, ..., B_i, !, B_j, ..., B_k.$$
$$H_2 :- B_m, ..., B_n.$$

Such clauses would be checked if Prolog attempts to satisfy an H goal. Notice the cut between goals B_i and B_j. The goals in the sequence $B_1, ..., B_i$ may backtrack amongst themselves, and if B_1 fails, then the second clause will be attempted. But now consider what happens if goal B_i succeeds. As soon as the 'cut' is crossed, the system is committed to the current choice of clause. All other choices are discarded. Goals $B_j, ..., B_k$ may backtrack amongst themselves, but if goal B_j fails, then the original H goal fails. The subsequent clauses will not be attempted.

Practice. Some of the following exercises are adapted from ones found in Ivan Bratko's book *Prolog Programming for Arificial Intelligence*.

1. Consider the following program:

   ```
   drink(milk).
   drink(beer) :- !.
   drink(gin).
   ```

   List all the answers to the following queries:

   ```
   ?- drink(X).
   ```

   ```
   ?- drink(X), drink(Y).
   ```

   ```
   ?- drink(X), !, drink(Y).
   ```

2. The following program classifies numbers into three mutually exclusive classes:

   ```
   class(N, pos) :- N > 0.
   class(0, zero).
   class(N, neg) :- N < 0.
   ```

Define this procedure in a way using cuts to make explicit the requirement that a classification is exclusive, that is, a number may not be reclassified into another class when backtracking occurs.

4.2   A Disjoint Partial Map with Cut

To illustrate the problems caused by the flexibility of expression that cut introduces, let's define several versions of the disjoint partial map split, which separates its input into the list of non-negative and negative numbers. The goal split(L, P, N) succeeds for list of numbers L, where P is the list of the non-negative numbers in L, and N is the list of the negative numbers in L.

1. *A version not using cut.* The following program is good code in the sense that each clause can be read on its own as one of the facts about the problem. However, it is not efficient because choice points are retained on each recursive call.

   ```
   split([], [], []).
   split([H|T], [H|Z], R) :- H >= 0, split(T, Z, R).
   split([H|T], R, [H|Z]) :- H < 0, split(T, R, Z).
   ```

Only one solution is obtained. If the H<0 goal were omitted from the third clause, alternative solutions might be obtained. Only the first solution is correct. One would be expected to ignore solutions subsequent to the first one. Insofar as this can be said to be a 'programming style' at all, this is the programming style used in this book before this chapter. If you look back through the previous programs, in some programs the 'guards' (such as H<0) have been included, and in others they have been omitted.

2. *A version using cut.* The next example is more efficient. However, it is not the best code, because the third clause will not stand independently as a fact about the problem. It needs to be read in the context of the procedure, as in ordinary programming languages. This style is often seen in practice, but it is not one to be encouraged.

```
split([], [], []).
split([H|T], [H|Z], R) :- H >= 0, !, split(T, Z, R).
split([H|T], R, [H|Z]) :- split(T, R, Z).
```

Even though the procedure may work efficiently as a functional unit, problems may arise during maintenance for the following reasons: (a) Having to be read in the context of the whole procedure, it is more difficult to understand what it does. (b) Minor modifications (such as adding more clauses) may have unintended effects.

3. *A version using cut which is also 'good code'* The only committal needed is after the sign of H has been ascertained in the second clause. The inefficiency is that the goal H < 0 will be executed unnecessarily whenever H < 0.

```
split([], [], []).
split([H|T], [H|Z], R) :- H >= 0, !, split(T, Z, R).
split([H|T], R, [H|Z]) :- H < 0, split(T, R, Z).
```

Many practitioners recommend this style for practical use.

There remains a hidden question concerning maintenance. If it is desired to add new clauses, the third clause as it stands does not capture the idea that H<0 is a committal. Here committal is the default because H<0 is in the last clause. To make the committal explicit, putting a cut on the third clause would be necessary:

```
split([], [], []).
split([H|T], [H|Z], R) :- H >= 0, !, split(T, Z, R).
split([H|T], R, [H|Z]) :- H < 0, !, split(T, R, Z).
```

However, anticipating such a maintenance requirement for a procedure which is already fully defined can be considered as unnecessary over-engineering.

4. *A version with unnecessary cuts*

```
split([], [], []) :- !.
split([H|T], [H|Z], R) :- H >= 0, !, split(T, Z, R).
split([H|T], R, [H|Z]) :- H < 0, !, split(T, Z, R).
```

Why is the cut in the first clause unnecessary? Because any goal matching the head of the first clause will not match anything else anyway. Most Prolog compilers will detect this. Why is the cut in the third clause unnecessary? Because H<0 is in the last clause. Whether or not H<0 fails, there are no choices left for the caller of split.

In general, when there is the opportunity to commit to a particular solution, it is wise to take the opportunity. This will be demonstrated in some of the following worksheets, which rework previous worksheets by including cut.

Here is a practical note. Standard Prolog makes available a deterministic 'if then else' predicate using the names '->' and ';'. Using this, max might be defined as:

```
max(X, Y, Z) :- X >= Y -> Z = X ; Z = Y.
```

Although the use of 'if then else' can lead to shorter and clearer programs, this book does not use it, so that underlying mechanisms can be exposed. For example, although 'if then else' can represent the decision that is needed for split, the desired effect of split is to construct two disjoint lists that are represented in the heads of separate clauses.

Worksheet 20: Multiple Choices with Cut

It is on page 31 that the need for committing to alternative choices becomes clear. Here is an another definition of squint which uses cut to commit to the first clause when the integer goal is satisfied:

```
squint([], []).
squint([X|T], [Y|L]) :- integer(X), !, Y is X * X, squint(T, L).
squint([X|T], [X|L]) :- squint(T, L).
```

Although the third clause still does not stand independently as a correct statement of the procedure (and therefore has the intended meaning only within the context of the whole procedure), the behaviour of the program during backtracking is now correct. Because the third clause is excluded whenever the cut goal succeeds, the third clause is not used when the goal backtracks.

Similarly, here is a definition of evens (see page 32) that uses cut to remove the need to make two mod tests, of which one is unnecessary:

```
evens([], []).
evens([X|T], [X|L]) :- 0 is X mod 2, !, evens(T, L).
evens([X|T], L) :- evens(T, L).
```

Similarly, here is a version of setify (see page 33) that uses cut to accomplish the same effect as was done for squint above:

```
setify([], []).
setify([X|T], L) :- member(X, T), !, setify(T, L).
setify([X|T], [X|L]) :- setify(T, L).
```

Set difference can be expressed as a partial map. The predicate sd is defined such that the goal sd(A, B, C) succeeds when set C is the result of subtracting set B from set A:

```
sd([], _, []).
sd([E | S1], S2, S3) :- membercheck(E, S2), !, sd(S1, S2, S3).
sd([E | S1], S2, [E | S3]) :- sd(S1, S2, S3).
```

Notice the standard pattern for a partial map. The membercheck predicate is the deterministic check for membership introduced at the beginning of this chapter. Even though membercheck will succeed at most once, if it does succeed it is necessary for sd to commit to that solution, hence the cut.

Worksheet 22: Ordered Search Trees

We can represent an ordered set in tree form. The tree consists of nodes n(A,L,R), where A is the (integer) item to be stored in the tree, L is a tree containing items smaller than A, and R is a tree containing items larger than A. We can use [] to terminate the branches of leaf nodes. Here is a typical tree.

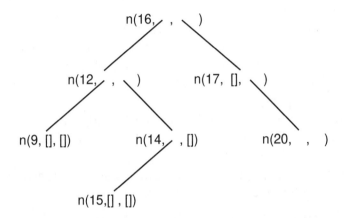

The location of nodes in the tree depends on the ordering relation (here integer less-than) and on the order in which nodes were inserted.

Insertion into an Ordered Tree

We want a program to insert items (integers) into an ordered tree. The desired predicate insert should be defined such that goals of the form insert(Item, OldTree, NewTree) cause Item (an integer) to be inserted in OldTree to give NewTree.

To program this, we need to recognise four cases:

- insertion into a nil tree: just grow a new leaf.
- the item is less than current node: just recur on the left-hand branch.
- the item is greater than current node: just recur on the right-hand branch.
- the item is the same as the current node: just return. The item has already been inserted.

We need a clause for each case.

Here is the wrong way to go about it, often attempted by beginners:

```
insert(I, [], n(I, [], [])).
insert(I, n(N, L, _), T) :- I < N, insert(I, L, T).
insert(I, n(N ,_, R), T) :- I > N, insert(I,R,T).
insert(I, n(I, _, _), _).
```

What is wrong with this? The problem is that although a new leaf is being constructed, the new tree is not being constructed by copying across each node of the old tree. To see the point of this, ask yourself what each clause puts into the third argument.

For a working program, it is necessary to copy each node of the tree as it is searched, so the whole tree (including the insertion) is in the output. We have also added cuts to render the procedure determinate:

```
insert(I, [], n(I, [], [])).
insert(I, n(N, L, R), n(N, L1, R)) :- I < N, !, insert(I, L, L1).
insert(I, n(N, L, R), n(N, L, R1)) :- I > N, !, insert(I, R, R1).
insert(I, n(I, L, R), n(I, L, R)).
```

Practice. The following unnecessary clauses are often added by beginners. Why are these clauses not necessary?

```
insert(I, n(N, [], R), n(N, n(I, [], []), R))  :- I < N, !.

insert(I, n(N, L, []), n(N, L, n([], I, []))) :- !.
```

It is good to be able to reason that special cases are subsumed by general cases.

Now that we know how to insert items, we now want to lookup items in the tree such that the goal lookup(Item, Tree) succeeds if the Item is in the Tree, and fails otherwise. What are the three cases? Give the clauses correspond to each case. Hint: lookup is a simplification of insert.

Worksheet 23: Frequency Distribution

Here is another scattered partial map with state. Given a list of keys (here just integers), find the frequency distribution of the keys, and sort the keys into order. We shall represent 'count c of key k' as the term $c*k$. Example:

?- freq([3, 3, 2, 2, 1, 1, 2, 2, 3, 3], A).

A = [2*1, 4*2, 4*3]

That is, there are two 1's, four 2's, and four 3's. So this is something like run-length encoding, but each output entry gives the count (frequency) of each key in the whole input list.

We define the predicate freq such that the goal freq(L, S) succeeds for data list L and frequency list S:

freq(L, S) :- freq(L, [], S).

freq([], S, S).
freq([N | L], S1, S3) :- update(N, S1, S2), freq(L, S2, S3).

The output list is modified using the update predicate, which is responsible for inserting the keys into the correct order.

/* update(Key, BeforeList, AfterList) */

update(N, [], [1*N]).
update(N, [F*N | S], [F1*N | S]) :- !, F1 is F + 1.
update(N, [F*M | S], [1*N, F*M | S]) :- N < M, !.
update(N, [F*M | S], [F*M | S1]) :- N \== M, update(N, S, S1).

Practice.   Explain why the presence of a cut renders the '\==' goal unnecessary in the fourth clause.

4.3 Taming Cut

It is not easy to understand the full implications of using cut. Programmers unfamiliar with cut often use it too much, in inappropriate
situations. Their programs 'die the death of a thousand cuts'. As Prolog
expert Richard O'Keefe says on page 96 of his book *The Craft of Prolog*,
the general rule is to place a cut

> ...precisely as soon as you know that this is the right
> clause to use, not later, and not sooner.

This wise advice is less tautologous than it sounds.

One way to domesticate the cut is to limit its use to special control
predicates. Here are some control predicates with their definitions.

The goal once(G) obtains and commits to the first solution of goal G.
It can be defined as follows:

```
once(G) :- call(G), !.
```

The goal for(N, G) executes goal G, N times. It is defined as follows:

```
for(0, G) :- !.
for(N, G) :- N > 0, call(G), M is N - 1, for(M, G), !.
```

The difficulty with using these control predicates is that they tend to
reinforce habits of thinking that are more suited to conventional
imperative languages. Sometimes, jumping too quickly to writing a
program using these control predicates can make one overlook a more
elegant formulation that is idiomatic to Prolog. For this reason, I avoid
using these control predicates.

4.4 Cut and Negation-as-Failure

Cut can be combined with the built-in predicate fail (which always fails)
and what somebody has called 'a casual disregard for the logical
independence of clauses' to generate a number of problems with using
cut. Consider the following examples.

1. John likes any food except beef:

```
likes(john, X) :- beef(X), !, fail.
likes(john, X) :- food(X).
```

2. A utility predicate meaning something like 'not equals'

```
different(X, X) :- !, fail.
different(X, Y).
```

Now consider a definition of the predicate not:

not(G) fails if G succeeds.

not(G) succeeds if G does not succeed.

Or in Prolog,

```
not(G) :- call(G), !, fail.
not(_).
```

Many Prolog systems have a built-in predicate like not. In Standard Prolog, it is written as \+. This does not correspond to logical negation, because it is based on the success or failure of goals. It can be useful, as in defining the above examples:

```
likes(richard, X) :- \+(beef(X)).

different(X, Y) :- \+(X = Y).
```

In Standard Prolog, a predicate equivalent to different is called \==, as seen earlier.

Practice. What is the behaviour of notmem, defined as:

```
member(X, [X|_]).
member(X, [_|T]) :- member(X, T).

notmem(X, L) :- \+(member(X, L)).
```

How does it compare with:

```
notmem1(X, []).
notmem1(X, [Y|T]) :- different(X, Y), notmem1(X, T).
```

4.5 Negation-as-Failure Can Be Misleading

Here is a story. Once upon a time yet to come, a student who did not read this book was commissioned to write a Police database system in Prolog. The database held the names of members of the public, distinguished by their known guilt or innocence in committing a particular crime. Suppose the database contained the following clauses:

```
innocent(peter_pan).
innocent(X) :- occupation(X, nun).
innocent(winnie_the_pooh).
innocent(julie_andrews).

guilty(X) :- occupation(X, thief).
guilty(joe_bloggs).
```

Consider the following dialogue concerning Saint Francis, whom everybody (except the Police database) knows to be innocent of any crime:

```
?- innocent(st_francis).
    no.
```

This cannot be right, because everyone knows that St Francis is innocent. But in Prolog the above happens because st_francis is not contained in the database. So the user believes that Saint Francis is not innocent. Because the database is hidden from the user, the user is likely to believe whatever the computer says, so the user believes that Saint Francis is guilty.

So on the evidence as reported by queries of this type, Saint Francis – along with several thousand other innocent people who are not in the database – are prosecuted for crimes they did not commit, and remanded into custody. After an enquiry lasting several years, the database program was investigated, and an attempt was made to remedy the shortcoming. The program was patched by defining:

    guilty(X) :- \+(innocent(X)).

But this is useless, and makes matters even worse, as we see here:

    ?- guilty(st_francis).
        yes.

It is one thing to show that st_francis cannot be demonstrated to be innocent. But is it quite another thing to claim that he is guilty.

Worksheet 24: Negation-as-Failure

Using cut to implement negation-as-failure can result in some disturbing behaviour, which is more subtle than the innocent/guilty problem and can lead to some extremely obscure programming errors. The following example is adapted from Ivan Bratko's book *Prolog Programming for Artificial Intelligence*. He uses restaurants and I use hotels run by famous logicians, but there is little difference otherwise.

Here is a database of hotels:

```
good_hotel(goedels).
good_hotel(freges).
good_hotel(schoenfinkels).
good_hotel(wittgensteins).

expensive_hotel(goedels).
expensive_hotel(wittgensteins).
```

And here is a predicate implementing a judgement about hotels, which uses the not predicate defined earlier:

```
reasonable(R) :- not(expensive_hotel(R)).
```

Consider the following dialogue:

```
?- good_hotel(X), reasonable(X).
    X = freges.
```

But if we ask the logically equivalent question:

```
?- reasonable(X), good_hotel(X).
    no.
```

Practice. Why do we get different answers for what seem to be logically equivalent queries? Hint: the difference between both questions is as follows. In the first question, the variable X is already instantiated when reasonable(X) is executed. In the second case, X is not instantiated.

It is bad practice to develop programs that destroy the correspondence between the logical and procedural meaning of a program without any good reason for doing so. Negation-as-failure does not correspond to logical negation, and therefore requires special care. One way to address the shortcoming posed by the above example is to specify that negation is undefined whever an attempt is made to negate a non-ground term. A ground term has no variables. That is, all variable symbols have been instantiated or 'bound'.

CHAPTER FIVE
DIFFERENCE STRUCTURES

The difference structure is a powerful data representation technique unique to Prolog. Difference structures simplify and increase the efficiency of programs by permitting 'partial' or 'incomplete' data structures to be specified and built up incrementally as the program executes. Variables are used as named 'holes' that can stand for parts of the data structure that are not yet computed. Difference structures are a generalisation of the idea of an accumulator. Where we have used accumulators to represent the 'result so far' during a computation, it is also possible for the idea of the accumulator to be extended to arbitrary data structures.

This chapter introduces difference structures, and particularly difference lists. One motivation for using difference lists is that it enables very efficient constant-time concatenation of lists. So, this chapter begins with the standard recursive method for concatenating lists, and then turns to difference lists.

Worksheet 25: Concatenating Lists

One of the most fundamental of operations over lists is concatenating them. The predicate append is defined such that the goal append (A, B, C) succeeds when C is the list obtained by concatenating A and B (or, in other words, appending B to A). The definition of append is one of the most elegant and succinct you will find, and understanding how append works is a big step towards mastering the use of variables. Here is an example of using append:

>   ?- append([a, b, c], [d, e, f], X).
>
>   X = [a,b,c,d,e,f]

Note that there is more to appending than simply 'cons'ing the lists together. If we mistakenly defined append as the clause

>   append(X,Y,[X|Y]).

this would simply produce the result [[a, b , c], d , e , f] when applied to the above query, which is not what is desired. The actual definition is as follows:

>   append([], L, L).
>   append([X|Y], T, [X|Z]) :- append(Y, T, Z).

The first clause specifies that if the first list is nil, the result is simply the second list. The second clause specifies that the next element of the output is simply the next element of the first list, followed by a list obtained by appending the rest of the first list to the second list. Don't worry if you feel you never could have invented this yourself.

Practice. What do the following goals do?

>   ?- append([a, b ,c], X, [a, b, c, d, e, f]).
>
>   ?- append(X, Y, [a, b, c, d, e, f]).
>
>   ?- append([[a,b,c]], [[d,e,f]], X).

You may be interested to know that this way of defining append is tail-recursive. Tail-recursive procedures have great benefits, as they can be executed with an efficiency comparable to that of iterative definitions. By contrast, the equivalent LISP or ML definition of append is not tail-recursive, because the last call is cons, not append.

Worksheet 26: Rotations of a List

To gain practice in appending lists, we shall now consider a puzzle in list processing. If you don't like puzzles, you can skip this worksheet without doing any harm.

   We need a definition of a procedure that will compute a list of all the rotations of a list. A list of length n has n rotations (including the identity rotation). Given the list $[x_1, x_2,..., x_n]$ for $n > 0$, the list of rotations should be the following list of lists

$$[[x_1, x_2, ..., x_n], [x_2, x_3, ..., x_n, x_1], ..., [x_n, x_1, x_2, ..., x_{n-1}]]$$

So for example, given [a, b, c], the list of all rotations is

   [[a, b, c], [b, c, a], [c, a, b]].

In Prolog this is easier to program than it sounds. We can use append. The goal rotate is defined such that the predicate rotall(X, Y, Z) succeeds for input list X, list of rotations Z, and accumulator Y. The accumulator is initialised to [] when the goal is called.

The definition is:

```
rotall([], A, []).
rotall([H|T], A, [L|Z]) :-
                append([H|T], A, L),
                append(A,[H],A1),
                rotall(T, A1, Z).
```

The key to this is to use the second argument as a state variable.

Practice. Work out what role the second argument plays by displaying the values of the first and second arguments for each recursive call, given the original goal

   ?- rotall([a, b, c, d], [], X).

It is possible to use an integer counter instead of a list in the second argument. How might you rewrite the procedure to use an integer counter? Using this technique it is sufficient to have one append goal.

Worksheet 27: Linearising

A fundamental operation similar to mapping is called linearising. Here we have an arbitrarily nested data structure as input, and we map this to an output as some linear sequence, in the form of a list. One case study that uses this involves the compilation of instruction sequences, for which the input is a parse tree of an expression, and the output is a sequence of the machine instructions that compute the expression.

But first, something easier: flattening lists. The input in this situation is an arbitrarily nested list, say

[a, [b,c], [d, e, [f, [g], h]]]

and we wish to construct an output list of all the elements of the input: [a, b, c, d, e, f, g]. The easiest way to do this is with append. We simply perform a depth-first search through the input list, and when we come to a constant, we append it to an accumulator. When we reach the end of the input, the output *is* the accumulator. The predicate flatten is defined such that the goal flatten(X, Y), succeeds for input list X and flattened output Y:

```
flatten([], []).
flatten([H|T], L3) :- flatten(H, L1,), flatten(T, L2), append(L1, L2, L3).
flatten(X, [X]).
```

The first clause flattens the null list to the null list. The second clause flattens a list by recursively flattening its head and tail, then joining the (flattened) results using append. The final clause handles non-list elements, which flatten into a list containing the element. The element needs to be enclosed as a list so that it is suitable to be appended.

That is the easy way, but it is very inefficient, particularly considering all those calls to append. Indeed, the same lists are appended over and over again with only minor differences between appends.

Practice. Given an input list of length *n*, how many calls to append are needed to flatten the list? Include the recursive calls to append. How many list cells are constructed?

There is another method, using what are sometimes called *difference lists*, which can be used for any linearising mapping. Performing linearising in this way is perhaps the most important and sophisticated Prolog programming technique, and using it makes all the difference between a 'toy' program such as flatten (as defined above) and an efficient program for a real application. We discuss this technique next.

5.1   Difference Lists

The idea of the difference list is to represent a list segment as a pair of terms, the *front* and the *back*. The front refers to the beginning of the list segment, and the back refers to the end of the segment. Often the back of a segment is a variable. If L1 and L2 are the front and back of a list segment respectively, then we call the pair of terms a difference list. For example, the list segment represented by the pair L1 and L2 contains the elements a, b, c, where the empty box depicts a variable:

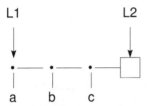

In Prolog this can be constructed by unifying L1 with [a,b,c | Z] and unifying L2 with Z. It is important that both Z's refer to the same variable. The variable to which L2 refers may be used as a 'hole' into which another term may be instantiated. If the other term is a difference list for which the back refers to a variable, then this becomes useful for concatenating list segments.

For example, suppose we wish to append the difference list made from L3 and L4 onto end of the difference list made from L1 and L2. The two list segments are shown here:

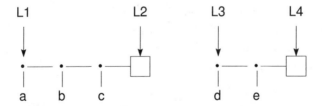

Because the result needs also to be a difference list, the result will be made from X and Y. Now the following are true about X and Y:

X should co-refer with L1 (to be the front of the list);

Y should co-refer with L4 (to be the back of the list);

L2 should co-refer with L3 (to join the lists together).

If the above co-references are accomplished, we get the diagram:

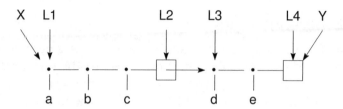

which is equivalent to:

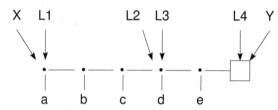

In Prolog we can use this idea to implement constant-time appending of two lists using difference lists. The goal app(L1, L2, L3, L4, X, Y) succeeds when the difference lists made from L1 and L2 and made from L3 and L4 are concatenated to form the difference list made from X and Y. As suggested above, carrying out this operation is simply a matter of rearranging variables. The definition of app is simply the single clause:

app(L1, L2, L2, L4, L1, L4).

An example execution:

?- app([a, b, c | Z1], Z1, [d, e |Z2], Z2, X, Y).

X = [a, b, c, d, e | Y].

Most Prolog systems will probably answer something equivalent like

X = [a, b, c, d, e | _265189], Y = _265189

It might be clearer to see the pattern involved in the rearrangement of variables if the definition of app is written as:

app(A, B, B, C, A, C).

This makes it clear that concatenating the segment from A to B with the segment from B to C gives the segment from A to C. We shall see that this will be a standard pattern in programs that use difference lists.

It is usual to denote difference lists by L1-L2, where '-' is a binary infix operator. This is called *difference notation*. This notation represents difference lists as a single term, and so cuts down on the arity of procedures. Programs are clearer, as in this definition of app using difference notation:

app(A-B, B-C, A-C).

Example:

　?- app([a, b, c | Z1]-Z1, [d, e | Z2]-Z2, X-Y).

　X-Y = [a, b, c, d, e | Y]-Y.

The only disadvantage is the space taken by the extra binary functors '-' that take part in the program. This is not a problem in practice.

Here is a summary of how to denote difference lists in Prolog. Suppose we use the difference notation. Then:

- L-L is the null difference list.

- [a | Z]-Z is the difference list containing 'a'. Similarly, [a, b, c | Z]-Z is the difference list containing a, b, and c.

- Unifying the difference list X with Y-[] will 'rectify' the list, that is, turn it into a proper list. For example, unifying [a, b, c | Z]-Z with Y-[] instantiates Y to [a,b,c].

Difference structures are very efficient and popular, in widespread use. They are also interesting because they are expressive of new methods of computation.

Difference structures can be misleading: Difference list **append** is not free of side-effects (but is backtrackable). Notice in the diagrams above that after the concatenation is performed, L1 and L2 have different values than they had before the concatenation. L1 now refers to the whole list, and L2 refers not to the back of the first segment, but to the front of the second segment. This goes against the principle that the values of inputs should not be changed by performing an operation. However, it is important to point out that backtracking is still able to undo the bindings, so this is not really a violation of the principle.

Difference structures are often hidden. Programmers can encapsulate the front and back of a list in a structure such as t(L1,L2). In common use for this purpose is the binary infix operator '-', for example L1-L2.

It might be useful to see the action of **app** as 'stitching together' two segments to make a longer segment, which in turn, has the correct structure to be stitched into a larger segment. But then, why bother use **app** when you can do the stitching 'in place' where it is needed in programs, simply by rearranging the variables in the clause! This is the basis of most advanced programming in Prolog, and will be covered in the following worksheets.

Worksheet 28: Linearising Efficiently

The purpose of linearising (see page 58) is to construct an output list, element by element, whenever we happen to have a new output element handy. The previous (inefficient) way was to append the new element to the end of the current output list, and the result takes over the place of the current output list.

Instead, consider the output list as being represented by a difference list X-Y. The front of the list is X; and Y stands for the back of the list: the place where a new element can be instantiated. Now whenever we have a new element handy, say H, we instantiate the second variable to the list cell [H|T], where T takes over the place of the second variable. Thus, we have a 'hole' T at the end of the list, with which we fill in a list cell containing the new element and another 'hole'. We can continue filling in holes like this until we come to the end of the input, in which case we fill the hole simply with a [] to terminate the list. In fact it is more common to terminate the list first, before the whole thing is constructed. This sounds very odd, but the next example demonstrates it.

The following shows how to program flatten using difference lists. The goal flatten(X, Y) flattens X to give Y, but now we use an auxiliary predicate. The predicate flatpair is defined such that the goal flatpair(X, L1-L2) succeeds for input list X, and the output list starts with L1 and ends with hole L2.

```
flatten(X, Y) :- flatpair(X, Y-[]).

flatpair([], L-L).
flatpair([H|T] ,L1-L3) :- flatpair(H, L1-L2), flatpair(T, L2-L3)
flatpair(X, [X|Z]-Z).
```

Look at flatpair. For the first clause, the nil case, the output list and hole are the same. In the second clause, we flatten the head and tail of the input, but we stitch together the holes at the end of each partial list in the order shown. In the third clause, we have a new element (X), so we construct the new list cell together with its new hole. You may need to work through this program using very short input lists to satisfy yourself of its operation. There is now an enormous gain in efficiency. Not only have we removed all the calls to append, but we have removed the need to construct partial output lists.

Practice. Given an input list of length n, how many list cells are created during the execution of the above program?

Worksheet 29: Linearising Trees

As we saw in the previous chapter, lists are special cases of binary trees: you can consider the binary functor '.' (the dot, or period, or full stop) as a node of the tree, with the head and tail as the branches. It is a special case because according the the theory of lists, the form of the right branch (the tail) is constrained (must be a list or []).

More generally, we can consider a binary tree as being constructed from a binary compound term n(*a*, *b*) called a node, where components *a* and *b* are either nodes or other terms. If a component of a node is a non-node, it is called a *leaf.*

Given a tree, it is often useful to gather information from the tree in the form of a list. We call this *linearising* a tree. As an example consider procedure lintree, defined here such that given tree X and list Y, goal lintree(X,Y) succeeds if Y is a list of all the integers found in X (with duplicates). Here is an inefficient definition based on the use of append. Note the use of the built-in predicate integer. The goal integer(X) succeeds if X is an integer.

```
lintree(n(A,B), L) :- lintree(A, LA), lintree(B, LB), append(LA, LB, L).
lintree(X, [X]) :- integer(X).
lintree(X, []).
```

Here is a better definition based on the use of difference lists as previously described:

```
lintree(X, Y) :- lindiff(X, Y-[]).

lindiff(n(A,B), L1-L3) :- lindiff(A, L1-L2), lindiff(B, L2-L3).
lindiff(X, [X|L]-L) :- integer(X).
lindiff(X, L-L).
```

Practice. You are given a tree which may contain the constants apple and pear (this is a rare genetically engineered fruit tree). Write a program to linearise the tree into a list of the apples and list of the pears such that the goal picktree(X, S, G) succeeds if S is a list of the apples and G is a list of the pears in tree X.

Worksheet 30: Difference Structures

Consider the task of normalising sum expressions. For example, the sums $(a+b)+(c+d)$ and $(a+(b+(c+d)))$ may be normalised into a standard form that associates on the left: $a+b+c+d$, or equivalently, $((a+b)+c)+d$. We wish to define a predicate normsum such that the goal normsum(X, Y) succeeds when the sum expression X normalises to Y.

One method is to flatten the sum, then build up in normalised form. However, we will see below that this can be done in one pass. Here is flat(A, B, C), which flattens the sum A into the difference list B-C:

    flat(X+Y, R1-R3) :- !, flat(X, R1-R2), flat(Y, R2-R3).
    flat(X, [X|Z]-Z).

The difference 'thread' is R1→R2→R3, and note the '!' to commit to the first clause when a sum node is encountered.

Normalising is not obvious. One solution is to accumulate 'the tree so far', and give it a new parent node each time an element is encountered. So we are 'stacking up' nodes instead of inserting them. We need a base case to terminate when the last element is encountered, and a '!' to commit to the solution. A base case for nil is not required because the flattened list will have at least two elements by definition. The 'tree so far' in the second argument needs to be initialised with the first element of the flattened list:

    build([X], T, T+X) :- !.
    build([H|L], T, Z) :- build(L, T+H, Z).

Thus, normalising X to get Y is defined by normalise(X,Y):

    normalise(A, C) :- flat(A, B-[]), B = [T|L], build(L, T, C).

However, it is perfectly possible to do both flattening and building in one pass, getting a better program:

    normalise(X, Y) :- norm(X, [], Y).

    norm(X+Y, A, C) :- !, norm(X, A, B), norm(Y, B, C).
    norm(X, [], X) :- !.
    norm(X, A, A+X).

Here the accumulator is used not only for differencing the elements, but also for building 'the tree so far'. The constant [] is used to represent the null accumulator, but there is no list processing as such.

Worksheet 31: Rotation Revisited

Let's return to the puzzle of rotating a list, this time using it as a vehicle for showing how useful it can be to apply simple algebraic transformations to programs.

Suppose we wish to rotate the elements of a list only by one element, so that

?- rot1([1,2,3], X).

$X = [2,3,1]$.

So by defining

rot2(X, Z) :- rot1(X, Y), rot1(Y,Z).

we could have

?- rot2([1,2,3], X).

$X = [3,1,2]$.

This can be done in an interesting way using difference lists, and it will illustrate a systematic way to develop programs in which the difference lists are constructed in-line.

To begin with, we are given the standard pattern for constant time appending of two difference lists:

app(X-Y, Y-Z, X-Z).

Can we define a rotate goal that uses this definition? Yes. A definition for rotate that uses app is:

rotate([A|B]-X, Y) :- app(B-X, [A|W]-W, Y).

So for example,

[a,b,c|Q]-Q → app([b,c|Q]-Q, [a|W]-W, X) → [b,c,a|X]-X.

The trick now is to simplify the above definition of rotate to eliminate the call to app, using the definition of app and simple rules for substituting variables. We obtain

rotate([A|B]-[A|W], B-W).

So now, using difference lists as input, we have

?- rotate([1,2,3|X]-X, Y).

$Y = [2,3,1|Q]-Q$.

Notice that the use of difference lists has no effect on the definition of rot2.

Practice. Give definitions of rot1 and rot2 in terms of rotate.

Worksheet 32: Max Tree

A *valued binary tree* (also called a *weighted* or *coloured* binary tree) can be defined using compound terms in the following way. A node of the tree is represented by the term n(v, l, r),where v stands for the value of the node (an integer in the range say $0 \le v \le 1024$) and l and r stands for the left and right branches, respectively. A terminal node will have l and r instantiated to []. Given some tree T, we say that its *greatest node* is the node in T with the maximum value of all nodes in T.

Practice. Given an input tree T, write a Prolog program that constructs a tree of the same shape as T, but in which the value of each node has been set to the value of the greatest node in T. For example, here is an input tree and its corresponding output tree:

INPUT:

n(3, n(1, n(4, [], []), n(1, [], [])), n(5, n(9, n(2, [], []), []), n(6, [], n(5, [], []))))

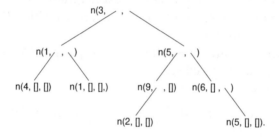

OUTPUT:

n(9, n(9, n(9, [], []), n(9, [], [])), n(9, n(9, n(9, [], []), []), n(9, [], n(9, [], []))))

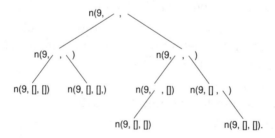

Hints: this task can be performed in *one* recursive descent of the input tree. The entire program need require no more than four clauses. Several accumulator variables are needed. The solution is on the next page. Don't look until you need help.

5.2   Solution to Max Tree

The key to solving the problem on the previous worksheet is to do as much as possible at the same time. Variables do the work for us. During the search of the input tree, when a node is encountered,

- a copy can be made for the output tree,
- the highest value so far can be accumulated, and
- a variable can stand for the value of the output tree's node. Eventually this variable, which must co-refer in all output nodes, will be unified with the highest value so far.

One program that illustrates this is as follows:

```
/* mt(InTree, OutTree) solves the max tree problem */
mt(A, B) :- mt(A, B, M, 0 ,M).


/* mt(InTree, OutTree, Hole, AccumHigh, Highest) */
mt(n(V,A,B), n(H,A1,B1), H, AC, N) :-
        V < AC,
        mt(A, A1, H, AC, ACA),
        mt(B, B1, H, ACA, N).
mt(n(V,A,B), n(H,A1,B1), H, AC, N) :-
        V >= AC,
        mt(A, A1, H, V, ACA),
        mt(B, B1, H, ACA, N).
mt([] ,[], _, A, A).
```

The first two clauses search the two possible subtrees below each node. Which choice to take depends on whether the value of the current node (V) is more or less than the highest value so far (AC). Notice that the AccumHigh accumulator is initialised to 0. Notice how Hole is put into each output node, and that eventually, AccumHigh is unified with Hole. Notice how the highest value so far is obtained from the left-hand branch of the tree, and this (ACA) is what is used to initialise the highest value so far in the right-hand branch of the tree.

Practice. The above definition uses, for tutorial purposes only, one more argument than procedure mt really needs. It is possible to reduce the number of arguments of mt by one. How?

CHAPTER SIX
CASE STUDY: TERM REWRITING

In this case study we shall look at various applications of term rewriting: symbolic differentiation, algebraic matrix products, and simplification. Most of the ideas illustrated in this case study will be used in subsequent case studies.

6.1 Symbolic Differentiation

This is a favourite example for non-numerical programming. You will find a symbolic differentiation program for almost any language that allows term rewriting. Versions can be found in LISP, POP-2, Snobol, and ML. Here it is in Prolog.

The goal d(A,B,C) means that C is the derivative of expression A with respect to variable B. Variables in the expression will be written as Prolog constants.

  d(X, X, 1).

  d(C, X, 0) :- atomic(C).

  d(-A, X, -U) :- d(A, X, U).

  d(A+B, X, U+V) :- d(A, X, U), d(B, X, V).

  d(A-B, X, U-V) :- d(A, X, U), d(B, X, V).

  d(A*B, X, B*U+A*V) :- d(A, X, U), d(B, X, V).

Now try finding the derivative of x^2-2 with respect to x:

  ?- d(x*x-2, x, X).

   $X = 1 * x + 1 * x - 0$

This is correct, but it might not look like what you had in mind, namely, $2x$. Here is why. The input expression has this structure:

Recursive descent of the input according to the above clauses will produce a similar shape structure for the output:

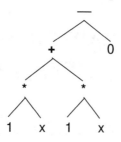

Each part of the tree has been rewritten according to the rules: 2 is rewritten to 0, and $x*x$ is rewritten to $(1*x)+(1*x)$. However, these operations have been carried out 'locally' within the tree. There is no opportunity to take advantage of possible further simplifications. It is necessary to subject the structure as a whole to algebraic simplification. We shall do this later. But first, here is another non-numerical exercise which will also motivate the need for simplification.

6.2 Matrix Products by Symbolic Algebra

In Prolog there is no real difference in program structure between analytic and numerical evaluation of matrix products, because the data movements are the same. This example will make use of inner product and transpose, introduced in a previous worksheet. As before, a matrix is represented as a list of lists. The relevant code is reproduced as follows:

```
/*  Product of two matrices  */
mm(A, B, C) :- transpose(B, BT), mmt(A, BT, C).

/*  Transpose a matrix  */
transpose([[] | _], []).
transpose(M, [Ci | Cn]) :- columns(M, Ci, R), transpose(R, Cn).
columns([], [], []).
columns([[Cii | Cin] | C], [Cii | X], [Cin | Y]) :- columns(C, X, Y).
```

/* Product of all rows of A with entire B */

mmt([] ,_, []).
mmt([Ai | An], B, [Ci | Cn]) :- mmc(Ai, B, Ci), mmt(An ,B, Cn).

/* Product of all "columns" of B with row A */

mmc(_, [], []).
mmc(A, [Bi | Bn], [Ci | Cn]) :- ip(A, Bi, Ci), mmc(A, Bn, Cn).

Only inner product, where the calculation is performed, needs to be modified. For an analytic product, the expression is passed as the result, instead of being evaluated. Predicate ip will succeed when for goal ip(A, B, X), X is a term describing the inner product of two vectors A and B:

/* Inner Product of two vectors */

ip([], [], 0).
ip([Ai | An], [Bi | Bn], (X + Ai * Bi)) :- ip(An, Bn, X).

For example, although we may calculate the inner product $[5,3]\cdot[2,7] = 210$, for the goal ip([5,3], [2,7], X), X will become instantiated to the algebraic (or analytic) equivalent term $0+(3*7)+(5*2)$.

Next, let's have some example matrices. You might recognise the following as the matrices for right-handed homogeneous transformations in three dimensions. We'll name them a, b, and c, and define them using the predicate ex, so that the goal ex(N, M) succeeds for the matrix M named N.

ex(a,   /* rotation by theta about the Y axis */

[[	cos(theta),	0,	-sin(theta),	0],
[	0,	1,	0,	0],
[	sin(theta),	0,	cos(theta),	0],
[	0,	0,	0,	1]]).

ex(b,   /* rotation by phi about the X axis */

[[	1,	0,	0,	0],
[	0,	cos(phi),	sin(phi),	0],
[	0,	-sin(phi),	cos(phi),	0],
[	0,	0,	0,	1]]).

```
ex( c,    /* rotation by psi about the Z axis */
    [[    cos(psi),    sin(psi),    0,    0],
     [   -sin(psi),    cos(psi),    0,    0],
     [    0,           0            1,    0],
     [    0,           0,           0,    1]]).
```

Example Run

If we multiply matrix a by matrix b, we should obtain a matrix that represents the composite transformation of a rotation about the Y axis followed by a rotation about the X axis:

?- ex(a, A), ex(b, B), mm(A, B, P)

P = [[0 + 0 * 0 + -(sin(theta)) * 0 + 0 * 0 + cos(theta) * 1, 0 + 0 * 0 + -(sin(theta)) * -(sin(phi)) + 0 * cos(phi) + cos(theta) * 0, 0 + 0 * 0 + -(sin(theta)) * cos(phi) + 0 * sin(phi) + cos(theta) * 0, 0 + 0 * 1 + -(sin(theta)) * 0 + 0 * 0 + cos(theta) * 0], [0 + 0 * 0 + 0 * 0 + 1 * 0 + 0 * 1, 0 + 0 * 0 + 0 * -(sin(phi)) + 1 * cos(phi) + 0 * 0, 0 + 0 * 0 + 0 * cos(phi) + 1 * sin(phi) + 0 * 0, 0 + 0 * 1 + 0 * 0 + 1 * 0 + 0 * 0], [0 + 0 * 0 + cos(theta) * 0 + 0 * 0 + sin(theta) * 1, 0 + 0 * 0 + cos(theta) * -(sin(phi)) + 0 * cos(phi) + sin(theta) * 0, 0 + 0 * 0 + cos(theta) * cos(phi) + 0 * sin(phi) + sin(theta) * 0, 0 + 0 * 1 + cos(theta) * 0 + 0 * 0 + sin(theta) * 0], [0 + 1 * 0 + 0 * 0 + 0 * 0 + 0 * 1, 0 + 1 * 0 + 0 * -(sin(phi)) + 0 * cos(phi) + 0 * 0, 0 + 1 * 0 + 0 * cos(phi) + 0 * sin(phi) + 0 * 0, 0 + 1 * 1 + 0 * 0 + 0 * 0 + 0 * 0]]

What a mess. The resulting expressions need to be simplified. This can be done by modifying inner product to construct simpler expressions, or by passing the result of mm to a simplifier. It is better to do the latter, partly to localise concerns, and partly because you would probably have to use the simplifier anyway.

6.3   The Simplifier

The idea is to recursively descend the expression tree, applying a simplification at each step. For example, the node A*1 can be simplified to B, where B is the simplified form of A. The obvious – but wrong – way to code this is to have a rule for each possible simplification, for example:

s(A*1, B) :- s(A, B).

And then we need rules to handle the general case for each operator. However, consider the general case:

```
s(A+B, U+V) :- s(A, U), s(B, V).
```

Suppose A simplifies to 1 and B simplifies to 0. Then this rule returns 1+0, which is not in simplest form.

Instead, at each node we need to descend each branch *and then* apply a simplification based on what the branches simplified to. This is what the following program does:

```
s(A+B, C) :- !, s(A, A1), s(B, B1), op(A1+B1, C).
s(A-B, C) :- !, s(A, A1), s(B, B1), op(A1-B1, C).
s(A*B, C) :- !, s(A, A1), s(B, B1), op(A1*B1, C).
s(X, X).

op(A+B, C) :- integer(A), integer(B), !, C is A+B.
op(0+A, A) :- !.
op(A+0, A) :- !.
op(1*A, A) :- !.
op(0*A, 0) :- !.
op(A*1, A) :- !.
op(A*0, 0) :- !.
op(A-0, A) :- !.
op(A-A, 0) :- !.
op(X, X).
```

Note the 'catchall' clauses at the end of each procedure. Why is there a cut for each op clause? To answer this question, consider what would happen if the goal op(0*0,Z) were given. There are three clauses that might match (including the catchall), and there is no point in using the catchall if a previous clause matches.

To actually simplify an expression, we need to take care of nega-'
tions first, by restricting the scope of a negation to only a constant or a variable. The predicate dn (for 'distribute negations') uses DeMorgan's Laws to push negations inwards:

```
dn(-(-(A)), B) :- !, dn(A, B).
dn(-(A+B), U+V) :- !, dn(-(A), U), dn(-(B), V).
dn(-(A*B), U*V) :- !, dn(-(A), U), dn(B, V).
dn(A+B, U+V) :- !, dn(A, U), dn(B, V).
dn(A*B, U*V) :- !, dn(A, U), dn(B, V).
dn(A, A).
```

```
/* simplify an expression */
simp(X, Y) :- dn(X, A), s(A, Y).
```

```
/* simplify each element of a matrix */
simplist([], []).
simplist([[H|T]|Z], [R|S]) :- !, simplist([H|T], R), simplist(Z, S).
simplist([H|T], [R|S]) :- simp(H,R), simplist(T, S).
```

Now let's try the matrix multiplication again, this time using the simplifier

```
?- ex(a,A), ex(b,B), mm(A,B,C), simplist(C, D).
```

D = [[cos(theta),-(sin(theta))* -(sin(phi)),-(sin(theta))*cos(phi),0],
[0,cos(phi),sin(phi),0], [sin(theta),cos(theta)* -(sin(phi)),
cos(theta)*cos(phi),0], [0,0,0,1]]

This is more like it. Formatting it nicely (and renaming theta and phi as the corresponding Greek characters so that longer expressions fit on the line), the resulting product is:

[[	$\cos(\theta)$,	$-(\sin(\theta))$* $-(\sin(\phi))$,	$-(\sin(\theta))$*$\cos(\phi)$,	0	],
[	0,	$\cos(\phi)$,	$\sin(\phi)$,	0	],
[	$\sin(\theta)$,	$\cos(\theta)$* $-(\sin(\phi))$,	$\cos(\theta)$*$\cos(\phi)$,	0	],
[	0,	0,	0,	1	]]

Bibliographic Notes

Other sources for symbolic differentiation can be found in the following textbooks:

Burstall, R.M., Collins, J.S. and Popplestone, R.J., 1977. *Programming in POP-2* (revised edition). Edinburgh University Press.

Clocksin, W.F. and Mellish, C.S., 1994. *Programming in Prolog* (4th edition), Springer-Verlag.

Griswold, R.E., Page, J.P. and Polonsky, I.P., 1971. *The SNOBOL4 Programming Language* (2nd edition). Prentice-Hall.

McCarthy, J, et al., 1962. *LISP 1.5 Programmer's Manual*. MIT Press.

Paulson, L.C., 1991. *ML for the Working Programmer*. Cambridge University Press.

Chapter Seven
Case Study: Manipulation of Combinational Circuits

One popular use of logic in computer science is the representation of boolean logic circuits, named after British mathematician George Boole (1815–1864). This case study will show one way in which Prolog can be used for the representation and manipulation of boolean logic circuits. We shall confine ourselves to combinational circuits (stateless logic functions). These are sometimes called 'combinatorial' circuits, but I prefer the term combinational partly because these circuits are combinations of boolean functions, and partly to distinguish the term combinatorial by its use in describing the complexity of algorithms.

Circuits having outputs that are also functions of internal state elements are called sequential circuits. Although Prolog can be used for representing sequential circuits, this is another topic with its own peculiarities, and will be considered in another case study starting on page 85.

7.1 Representing Circuits

There are many possible ways to represent circuits. It is necessary to represent primitive components of the technology. These may be discrete components such as resistors or capacitors, or more complex components such as logic gates. There must be a way to connect the components together, and a way to encapsulate a circuit, which makes it explicit as an individual component having inputs and outputs to which other components can be connected.

First consider the common logic gates, which may be represented as relations between their inputs and outputs as illustrated here:

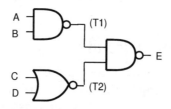

inv(A, B)   or(A, B, C)

and(A, B, C)   xor(A, B, C)

nand(A, B, C)   nor(A, B, C)

It is conventional to write inputs before outputs, so that, for example, nand(A,B,C) has inputs A and B, and output C.

Knowing the truth-table definitions for these logic functions, the corresponding procedures can be defined in the expected way:

inv(0, 1).
inv(1, 0).

nand(0, 0, 1).
nand(0, 1, 1).
nand(1, 0, 1).
nand(1, 1, 0).

and so forth.

Circuits may be built up by constructing Prolog procedures containing goals for representing circuit elements. Here is the schematic for a simple combinational logic function:

A
B   (T1)

                          E

C
D   (T2)

Assuming suitable definitions for nand and nor, this circuit may be defined as:

```
c1(A, B, C, D, E) :-
        nand(A, B, T1),
        nor(C, D, T2),
        nand(T1, T2, E).
```

Note that the 'internal' nodes for connecting to the inputs of the final NAND gate are called T1 and T2.

Inputs may be shared simply by naming the input with the same variable:

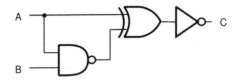

c2(A, B, C) :-
      nand(A, B, T1),
      xor(A, T1, T2),
      inv(T2, C).

And internal nodes are just as easily shared:

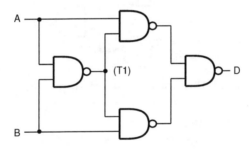

c3(A, B, D) :-
      nand(A, B, T1),
      nand(A, T1, T2),
      nand(B, T1, T3),
      nand(T2, T3, D).

The next example shows the full power of procedural abstraction. A three-bit subtracter[1] is composed from a half-subtracter and two full subtracters. The half-subtracter half_sub(I1,I2,D,BO) has inputs I1 and I2, and outputs difference D and 'borrow out' BO:

---

1. In case you find this spelling unfamiliar, a 'subtracter' is a device that subtracts. 'Subtractor' describes something below a tractor.

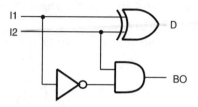

half_sub(I1, I2, D, BO) :- xor(I1, I2, D), inv(I1, T1), and(I2, T1, B).

The full subtracter full_sub(I1,I2,BI,D,BO) has inputs I1 and I2, 'borrow in' BI, difference D and 'borrow out' BO:

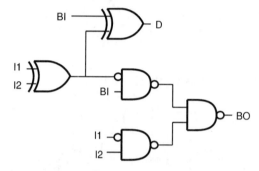

Notice we have used the convention of duplicating terminal names instead of drawing lines. The procedure looks like this:

full_sub(I1, I2, BI, D, BO) :-
        xor(I1, I2, T1), xor(T1, BI, D), inv(T1, T2), inv(I1, T3),
        nand(T2, BI, T4), nand(T3, B, T5), nand(T4, T5, BO)).

Finally, the three-bit subtracter simply refers to the other definitions as goals. The procedure three_sub(A0,A1,A2,B0,B1,B2,D0,D1,D2,T2) has three bits of A input A0, A1, A2; three bits of B input B0, B1, B2; three bits of difference output D0, D1, D2; and 'borrow out' T2:

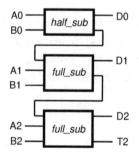

```
three_sub(A0,A1,A2,B0,B1,B2,D0,D1,D2,T2) :-
            half_sub(A0,B0,D0,T0),
            full_sub(A1,B1,T0,D1,T1),
            full_sub(A2,B2,T1,D2,T2).
```

Combinational circuits of arbitrary complexity may be composed in this manner.

7.2   Simulation of Circuits

Now that we can represent circuits, one useful task is the simulation (or evaluation or sometimes inaccurately called abstract interpretation) of circuits. Given values for the inputs to a given circuit, it is possible to calculate the circuit's output by evaluating each component of the circuit simply by executing it as a Prolog program. Because connections are represented as variables, it is not even necessary to know all the input values, and so 'hypotheses' are formed about any unknown values. If the assumed value is inconsistent with a value later in the evaluation, backtracking will cause another value to be hypothesised.

For example, with procedure c3 as defined above, we can pose the following query to establish the conditions for the validity of c3:

?- c3(A, B, Q).

    A = 0, B = 0, Q = 0 ;

    A = 0, B = 1, Q = 1 ;

    A = 1, B = 0, Q = 1 ;

    A = 1, B = 1, Q = 0 ;

    no

This goal has four solutions, which enumerate the possible assignments of boolean values to the 'free' input variables A and B and the free output Q. As you can see, c3 is revealed as being equivalent to the exclusive-or function.

7.3   Sums and Products

With the advent of programmable logic arrays, there is less need to design and manipulate random circuitry. Digital designers can write a set of expressions in which the legal connectives are sums (representing or), products (representing and) and negations (representing not). The reason we might wish to automatically manipulate such expressions is to convert them into a standard form, such a 'sum of products standard form' (or SOP standard form) that reflects the internal architecture of programmable logic arrays. Let us use terms of the form -X, X+Y, and X*Y to represent negation, summation, and multiplication respectively. These are often seen in electronics texts written as $\overline{X}$, X+Y, and XY respectively. An expression E made up from these terms is said to be in SOP standard form if it is accepted by the following grammar:

Exp ← Product + Product +...+ Product

Product ← Literal * Literal *...* Literal

Literal ← Atom | -Atom

Atom ← *constant* | *variable*

Round brackets are permitted for grouping. So for example, the expression a*b+(-a)+b*c is in SOP standard form. Ordinary Prolog syntax may be used to construct expressions of this form.

There is a two-step process for converting an arbitrary expression into SOP standard form. First we use De Morgan's laws (due to Augustus De Morgan (1806–1871), British mathematician and eccentric) to reduce the scope of negation, so that any negations in the input expression are rewritten to apply only to a constant or variable.

The procedure dm is defined such that the goal dm(X,Y) converts an expression X into a 'DeMorganised' form Y, in which the scope of negations has been minimised. In the same way as for the algebraic simplifier in an earlier case study (page 72), this proceeds by recursive descent, and the inputs to an operator need to be demorganised before the operator itself can be. The definition of dm is as follows:

```
dm(0, 0).
dm(1, 1).
dm(-(-A), B) :- dm(A, B).
dm(-(A+B), U*V) :- dm(-A, U), dm(-B, V).
dm(-(A*B), U+V) :- dm(-A, U), dm(-B, V).
dm(A+B, U+V) :- dm(A, U), dm(B, V).
dm(A*B, U*V) :- dm(A, U), dm(B, V).
dm(X, X).
```

The final clause is a 'catchall' so that variables and constants will be accepted. For example,

```
?- dm(-(a*b)+a*(-(b+c)), X).

X = -(a)+ -(b)+a*(-(b)* -(c))
```

The next step is to convert the demorganised term into SOP form. The program uses two mutually recursive procedures. The procedure **sop** searches the arguments of each kind of operator, distributing products over sums when necessary. The procedure **dist** actually does the distribution by multiplying through products where necesssary, ensuring that the products are expressed in SOP standard form.

```
sop(P*Q, R) :- sop (P, P1), sop (Q, Q1), dist(P1*Q1, R).
sop (P+Q, P1+Q1) :- sop (P, P1), sop (Q, Q1).
sop(X,X).
dist( (P+Q)*R, P1+Q1) :- sop(P*R, P1), sop (Q*R ,Q1).
dist(P*(Q+R), Q1+R1) :- sop(P*Q, P1), sop (P*R, R1).
dist(P,P).
```

For example,

```
| ?- dm((a+b)*(-a+b),A), sop(A, B).
    A = (a+b)*(-(a)+b),
    B = a* -(a)+a*b+(b* -(a)+b*b)
```

Finally, although expressions output from sop may now be in SOP standard form, there is the possibility that the sum is not linearised: that is, expressions of the form (P+P)+(P+P) may have been constructed, as seen in the above answer. Instead, for convenience of subsequent processing, it is useful to represent SOP expressions in a linear form using lists according to the following grammar:

Exp ← [Product, Product, ..., Product]

Product ← [Literal, Literal, ..., Literal]

Literal ← Atom | -Atom

Atom ← *constant* | *variable*

For example, the SOP expression a*b+(-a)*c+b*c can be represented as [[a,b], [-a,c],[b,c]].

The way to do this is simply to 'flatten' the sum tree into a list, and gather up the products into a list when they are found. In the following program, flat(X,Y) takes the SOP expression X which is possibly not in flattened form, and converts it to a list Y. The difference list technique is used to construct Y. When factors are encountered, they are put into a list, ensuring that duplicates are removed, by goal setfactors(A,B). List (or actually set) B is constructed by accumulation, initialised to the nil list.

```
flat(A+(B+C),U) :- !, flat((A+B)+C,U).
flat(A+B,L1-L3) :- !, flat(A,L1-L2), flat(B,L2-L3).
flat(A,[B|Q]-Q) :- setfactors(A, [], B).

setfactors(A*B, Acc, L) :- !, setfactors(A, Acc, A1), setfactors(B, A1, L).
setfactors(A, L, [A|L]) :- notin(A,L), !.
setfactors(A, L, L).
```

Duplicates are checked by procedure notin, which tests whether A is not in the list L, and is defined

```
notin(X,[]) :- !.
notin(X, [Y|T]) :- X \== Y, notin(X,T).
```

For example, taking the SOP expression found above, and remembering that the solution is given as a difference list, we have

```
?- flat(a* -(a)+a*b+(b* -(a)+b*b), L-[]).

    L = [[-(a),a],[b,a],[-(a),b],[b]]
```

Note how the last list is [b], and not [b,b], because notin has removed the duplicate.

7.4   Simplifying SOP Expressions

One useful simplification of an SOP expression is to remove products that contain both a variable and its negation. This follows from the theorems that for boolean A and B, $-A*A=0$, and $B+0=B$. So for example, the expression

$$a*b+(-a)*c*a+b*c$$

can be simplified to $a*b+b*c$. Using the 'flat' list notation, the procedure simp(X, Y) will simplify the SOP expression X, removing all redundant products, giving output Y.

```
simp([], []).
simp([P|L], L1) :- zero(P), !, simp(L, L1).
simp([P|L], [P|L1]) :- simp(L, L1).
```

You should recognise this as a partial map. Redundancy of a product is tested by zero, which checks to see whether the negation of a term is found. The demorganiser defined in the previous section is called to ensure that the negated term is reduced to lowest terms:

```
zero([H|T]) :- dm(-H, H1), membercheck(H1, T).
```

The member goal is the deterministic check for membership:

```
membercheck(X, [X|_]) :- !.
membercheck(X, [_|T]) :- membercheck(X, T).
```

So for example,

```
?- simp([[-(a),a],[b,a],[-(a),b,a],[b]], L).

    L = [[b,a],[b]]
```

Another useful simplification of an SOP expression is to remove redundant products. This follows from the theorem that for boolean A and B, $A+A*B=A$. We can eliminate redundant products using this theorem as follows. Take each term in succession and compare with it all products containing fewer factors. The given term is not included in the output list if it contains all the factors of another term. Another way to phrase this is that if in an SOP expression we find two products P and Q, we wish to remove any product P for which Q is a proper subset of P. Here the procedure purge does this removal. For goal purge(X, Y, Z, A), if X is a list, and Y is a list of lists, then Z is obtained by excluding from Y those elements with X as a proper subset. Furthermore, A will be set to [X] if X is in Y, else A will be []. Goals for purge are called from purge_all, which in turn is called from remove:

    remove(A, B) :- purge_all(A, [], A, B).

    purge_all([], [], X, X).
    purge_all([], [A], X, [A|X]).
    purge_all([H|T], [], E, R) :- purge(H, E, R1, A), purge_all(T, A, R1, R).
    purge_all([H|T], [A], E, R) :-
                        purge(H, [A|E], R1, B), purge_all(T, B, R1, R).

    purge(_,[],[],[]).
    purge(X, [X|T], Z, [X]) :- !, purge(X, T, Z, _).
    purge(X, [Y|T], Z, A) :- subset(X, Y),!, purge(X, T, Z, A).
    purge(X, [Y|T], [Y|Z], A) :- purge(X, T, Z, A).

The definition for subset is straightforward:

    subset([], _).
    subset([X|T], Y) :- membercheck(X, Y), subset(T, Y).

This program also removes duplicates, as can be seen by the following example:

    ?- reduce([a], [b,c], [a, -c, b], [b,c]], A).

      L = [[a], [b,c]]

7.5 Alternative Representation

This case study has proceeded from general operations on arbitrary expressions to specific operations on expressions written in a special form. When this happens it is always wise to consider that suitable methods might favour a different data structure for expressions. For example, suppose all our expressions have at most n distinct variable names (and here suppose $n=4$). Depending on the application, it might be worth representing a product as the term p(_, _, _, _) where each argument of term p represents the same variable name (say in the order w, x, y, z), and is either + (for $+x$), - (for $-x$), or 0 (for not used). The SOP standard form expression

$(-w)^*(-x)^*y^*x + (-w)^*z + (-w)^*(-x)^*(-y)^*(z)$

or, in conventional electronics usage, $\overline{W}XYZ + \overline{W}Z + \overline{WXY}Z$, might then be written as

$[p(-,-,+,+), p(-,0,0,+), p(-,-,-,+)].$

Or, another alternative is to use a list format, written as

$[p([-,-,+,+]), p([-,0,0,+]), p([-,-,-,+])]$

Exercises

1. Arrive at an understanding of purge and purge_all.

2. Rewrite the SOP examples using an alternative representation as suggested in Section 7.5.

Bibliographic Notes

The modelling and simulation of combinational circuits in Prolog is discussed in:

W.F. Clocksin, 1987. Logic programming and digital circuit analysis. *Journal of Logic Programming* **4**, 59-82.

from which the examples in Section 7.1 were drawn. My colleague Ian Lewis rewrote and improved the examples that now appear in Section 7.4.

CHAPTER EIGHT
CASE STUDY: MANIPULATION OF CLOCKED SEQUENTIAL CIRCUITS

A previous case study showed how Prolog can be used for direct simulation of combinational circuits. We now turn to the problem of clocked sequential circuits. There are two issues to define first. It is only possible to model sequential circuit components because we are willing to make some assumptions about (a) their internal state and (b) their timing delays. We shall use a very simple model in which each component will be responsible for representing its own internal state, and all delays will be of unit duration. Every component will be synchronised by the same clock. The clock can be represented simply as a list of pulses, for example the list [1, 1, 1, 1, 1] shows five pulses of the clock signal.

Let's begin with the simplest sequential component, the D-type flip-flop. The term dff(D,C,Q,N) represents the D-type flip-flop with input D, clock C, output Q, and next state N. For convenience, we have left out the negated output which is available on some devices. The two clauses defining dff are:

dff(D, 0, Q, Q).

dff(D, 1, Q, D).

The first clause specifies the behaviour on a falling clock: the next state is the same as the current state. The second clause specifies behaviour on a rising clock: the next state is the same as the D input.

8.1   Divide-by-Two Pulse Divider

The simplest sequential circuit is a divide-by-two pulse divider, having
the following schematic:

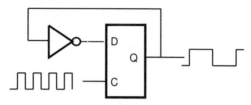

The pulse divider can be specified as follows, with the inv predicate
implementing a simple inverter:

    inv(0, 1).
    inv(1, 0).

    div(C, Q, Z) :- inv(Q, D), dff(D, C, Q, Z).

The goal div(C, Q, N) has clock input C, a current state Q, and a next
state N. We can insert this module into a 'test circuit' by writing a
procedure that recurs over an input list of clock pulses. The initial state
of the circuit can be initialised to 0, and the output states can be
collected into a list. The goal divide(P, S, Q), when given a clock pulse
list P and initial state S, will construct an output list Q. The definition
of divide is:

    divide([], _, []).

    divide([P|Ps], S, [Q|Qs]) :- div(P, S, Q), divide(Ps, Q, Qs).

According to the terminology introduced in the worksheets, this is a full
map. Sample executions follow:

    ?- divide([1,1,1,1,1,1], 0, Q).
       Q = [1, 0, 1, 0, 1, 0]
    ?- divide([0, 1, 0, 0, 1, 1, 0, 0, 0, Q).
       Q = [0, 1, 1, 1, 0, 1, 1, 1].

8.2   Sequential Parity Checker

The next circuit is a sequential parity checker. On each clock pulse, the
output provides an odd-parity check on however many data bits have
been received by the serial input since the initial state of the circuit was
set. The schematic looks like this:

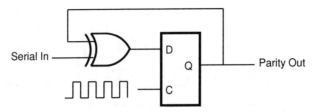

The sequential parity checker is specified by the predicate par(C,D,Q,N) for clock input C, serial data input D, parity output Q, and next state N, using the following definition, including a definition of the xor function:

    xor(0, 0, 0).
    xor(0, 1, 1).
    xor(1, 0, 1).
    xor(1, 1, 0).
    par(Clock, X, Z, Z1) :- xor(X, Z, T), dff(X, Clock, Z, Z1).

We can use the technique of mapping over a list of clock pulses to form a test circuit parity(C, S, N, Q) for clock pulse list C, serial input list S, initial state N, and serial parity output S:

    parity([], S, N, []).
    parity([C|Cs], [S|Ss], N, [Z|L]) :- par(C, S, N, Z), parity(Cs, Ss, Z, L).

When the initial state is initialised (or in electronics parlance 'jammed') to 0, an example goal is as follows:

    ?- parity([1,1,1,1,1,1], [1,0,0,1,1,0], 0, Q).
        Q = [1,1,1,0,1,1].

Note that, for the given input, odd parity is counted for the first three and the last two clock pulses.

8.3 Four-Stage Shift Register

The next example is a four-stage shift register, in which the output follows the input delayed by four clock pulses. What is illustrated here is how to manage the state variables of several components using one data structure. The shift register is constructed from D-type flip-flops, and has the following schematic:

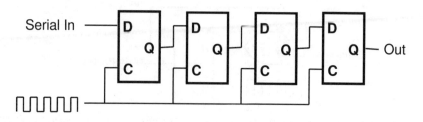

We shall represent the state of the circuit as a term s(F1, F2, F3, F4), where the current state of each flip-flop is represented as one of the arguments of s. The four-stage shift register is specified by the predicate sh4(C, D, Q, N) for clock input C, serial data input D, current state Q, and next state N, using the following definition:

        sh4(C, D, s(Q1,Q2,Q3,Q4), s(N1,N2,N3,N4)) :-
                            dff(D, C, Q1, N1),
                            dff(Q1, C, Q2, N2),
                            dff(Q2, C, Q3, N3),
                            dff(Q3, C, Q4, N4).

We can use the technique of mapping over a list of clock pulses to form a test circuit shifter(C, S, A, Z) for clock pulse list C, serial input list S, input state A, and serial output list Z. On each clock pulse, it is necessary to initialise the input state with the next state. This is done simply by passing the s term to the next recurrence of shifter:

        shifter([], _, _, []).
        shifter([C|Cs], [S|Ss], A, [Q|L]) :-
                            sh4(C, S, A, N),
                            N = s(_, _, _, Q),
                            shifter(Cs, Ss, N, L).

Notice that the serial output Q is obtained by extracting the state of the fourth flip-flop. When the initial state is jammed to s(0, 0, 0, 0), an example goal is as follows:

        ?- shifter([1,1,1,1,1,1,1,1,1,1], [1,0,0,1,1,0,0,1,1,1], s(0,0,0,0), L).
            L = [0,0,0,1,0,0,1,1,0,0]

Although informally we say that the serial input is delayed by four clock pulses, we see here the correct behaviour that the first bit of the serial input appears at the output coinciding with the (falling edge of the) fourth clock pulse.

8.4 Gray Code Counter

The next example puts together some combinational and sequential circuitry, showing how circuit design can be modularised. A Gray code is a binary encoding of the integers in which the encoding of successive integers differs by only one bit. There are many possible Gray codes. Here is one possible Gray code for the first eight integers:

001, 011, 010, 110, 111, 101, 100, 000.

A schematic of a three-bit Grey code counter is shown here:

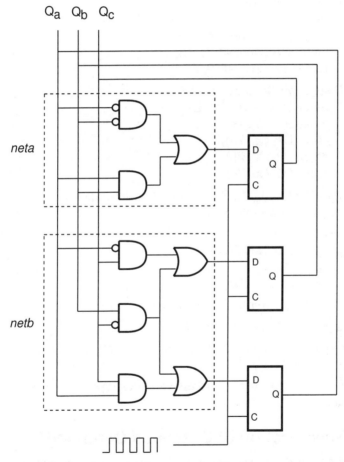

Here two combinational modules are specified as separate clauses for procedures neta and netb shown outlined in the schematic. The and and or procedures are defined in the expected way, and inv and dff are defined above. A state vector for the circuit is represented by the term s(Qa, Qb, Qc) in which the state for each flip-flop is stored. Notice that the clauses for and and or are placed along the line to save paper.

```
and(0, 0, 0).  and(0, 1, 0).  and(1, 0, 0).  and(1, 1, 1).
or(0, 0, 0).   or(0, 1, 1).    or(1, 0, 1).    or(1, 1, 1).


neta(A, B, Q) :-
        and(A, B, T1),
        inv(A, NA), inv(B, NB), and(NA, NB, T2),
        or(T1, T2, Q).
netb(A, B, C, Q1, Q2) :-
        and(A, C, T1),
        inv(C, NC), and(B, NC, T2),
        inv(A, NA), and(NA, C, T3),
        or(T1, T2, Q1), or(T2, T3, Q2).
gcc(C,s(Qa,Qb,Qc),s(Za,Zb,Zc)) :-
        netb(Qa, Qb, Qc, D1, D2),
        neta(Qa, Qb, D3),
        dff(C, D1, Qa, Za),
        dff(C, D2, Qb, Zb),
        dff(C, D3, Qc, Zc).
```

A test circuit testgcc(C, N, S) is defined which takes a clock pulse list C, a state vector S, and next state N.

```
testgcc([],_,[]).
testgcc([C|Cs],S,[N|Ns]) :-
        gcc(C, S, N),
        testgcc(Cs, N, Ns).
```

A query to test the circuit for nine pulses is

```
?- testgcc([1,1,1,1,1,1,1,1,1], s(0,0,0), Q).
```

Q = [s(0,0,1), s(0,1,1), s(0,1,0), s(1,1,0), s(1,1,1), s(1,0,1), s(1,0,0), s(0,0,0), s(0,0,1)]

It can be observed that the successive states represent an incrementing Gray code.

8.5   Specification of Cascaded Components

The final example shows how recursion can be used to specify a cascade of components parametrically. A *unit delay* is a sequential component whose output follows its input delayed by one clock pulse. The procedure unit(A, S, N) is defined for input A, current state S, and next state N:

    unit(0, 0, 0).
    unit(1, 0, 1).
    unit(0, 1, 0).
    unit(1, 1, 1).

A special feature of this definition is that there is no explicit clock input; it is assumed that input pulses are synchronised with the clock. A unit delay is a simplification of a D-type flip-flop. Indeed, you can confirm this by by deriving the definition of unit from the definition of dff, assuming the clock input will always be 1.

We may now connect n unit delays in series to produce an n-delay component as depicted here:

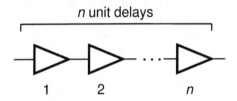

Each unit delay requires one bit of state, which implies the need for a state n-vector for an n-delay component. Because the actual number of unit delays is a parameter of the definition, it is best to represent the n-delay component's state n-vector by a list of length n. The procedure delay(A,S,Q,N), is defined for input A, current state n-vector S, output Q and next state n-vector N:

    delay(A, [], A, []).

    delay(A, [S|Ss], Q, [Z|Zs]) :- unit(A, S, Z), delay(S, Ss, Q, Zs).

In this definition, the number of delays to cascade is given by the length of list S, so the n-delay component is constituted by recursion over the length of S. This component may be placed in a test procedure test(P, S, Q), where P is the input pulse list, S is an initial state n-vector, and Q is the output pulse list:

    test([], S, []).

    test([P|Ps], S, [Q|Qs]) :- delay(P, S, Q, Z), test(Ps, Z, Qs).

A query to test the circuit delaying by three clock cycles a pulse list occupying eight clock cycles is:

    ?- test([1,1,0,0,1,1,0,0], [0,0,0], Q).

    Q = [0,0,0,1,1,0,0,1]

Exercises

1. Using the definition of dff as shown above, produce an *n*-bit shift register using the technique of parametric specification of cascaded components.

2. Prove that unit is a special case of dff.

3. Give a one-clause definition of unit equivalent to the one shown above.

Bibliographic Notes

The modelling and simulation of sequential circuits in Prolog is discussed in:

W.F. Clocksin, 1987. Logic programming and digital circuit analysis. *Journal of Logic Programming* **4**, 59-82.

from which the examples in this chapter were drawn.

CHAPTER NINE
CASE STUDY: A COMPILER FOR THREE MODEL COMPUTERS

The purpose of a compiler is to translate a program in the source language to a program in a target language. Usually the source program is written in a high-level programming language, and the target program is an assembly listing for a particular computer. Because compilation is often considered as a recursive task that transforms one data structure into another, compilation is a natural application for Prolog. Most Prolog compilers and interpreters are written in Prolog.

With Prolog it is easy to arrange the kind of expression manipulation and tree transformation necessary for most compilation tasks. This was demonstrated in David H.D. Warren's article from 1980, which has inspired some of the examples in this chapter. There are more details about David Warren's article in the bibliographic notes at the end of this chapter.

But it is possible to go beyond this. Prolog's rule-based approach makes it easy to express complicated, ad hoc operations such as strength reduction and peephole optimisations. In this Case Study we shall see how Prolog can be applied to several typical compilation tasks. To make the treatment more general than is found in other books, we shall consider compilation tasks for three different computer architectures: a single-accumulator computer, a reduced instruction set computer (RISC), and a stack machine.

Compilation is performed in a number of successive stages as shown here:

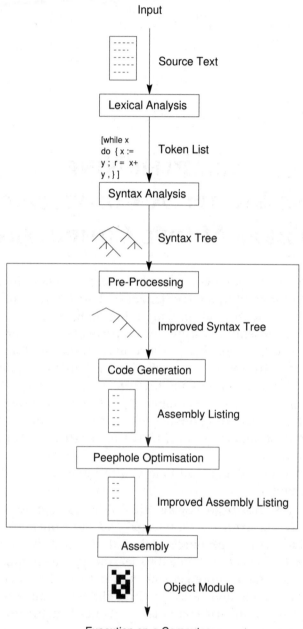

In this case study we shall consider only the three most interesting stages, code generation and the two improvement stages, as shown inside the big box on the previous diagram.

Here is a simple source program fragment which assigns to r the factorial of n:

```
c := 1;
r := 1;
while c < n do (c := c + 1;   r := r * c)
```

Note that the source language is similar to PASCAL, except that round brackets are used instead of the words begin and end. Also note that the semicolon is used as a separator, and not as a terminator.

To generate an assembly listing from the source program, the program is translated by the first three stages of the compiler into a syntax tree. Each syntactic construct of the source language corresponds to a Prolog compound term, which can be considered as the node of a syntax tree. Some correspondences are shown here:

Source Language Construct	Corresponding Prolog Term
$x := y$	assign(x, y)
while x do y	while(x, y)
$x ; y$	$x ; y$
$x < y$	$x < y$
$x + y$	$x + y$
$x * y$	$x * y$

Note that some of the compound terms are written in the infix form, in particular the sequence construct ';', and the arithmetic and comparison operators. These terms have built-in infix declarations in standard Prolog.

The above program can be parsed into the following syntax tree represented as a Prolog term:

assign(c,1) ; assign(r,1) ; while(c < n, (assign(c, c+1) ; assign(r, r + 1)))

And here is a graphic depiction of the syntax tree:

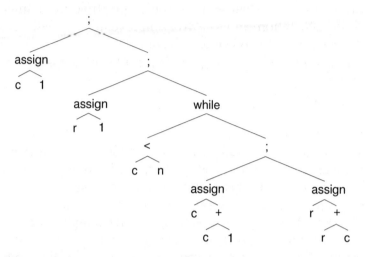

The code generator will translate this syntax tree into an assembly language listing for the target model computer.

The model computer shown in the following diagram is typical of many real computers:

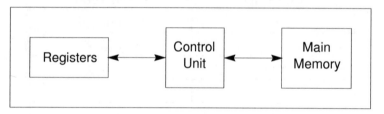

Instructions and data are stored in the *main memory*. Instructions are executed by the *control unit,* and temporary results are stored in a small set of *registers*. We shall consider three different target computers based on this model:

- A computer having many fast registers. Arithmetic operations refer only to registers. This design is characteristic of modern 'reduced instruction set' computers.

- A computer having only one register called the accumulator. Arithmetic operations refer to the accumulator and to an argument in the main memory. This design is characteristic of early computers such as the PDP-8 and some microprocessors.

- A 'stack machine' computer having no explicit registers. Arithmetic operations refer to a first-in-last-out stack onto which arguments and results are pushed.

The details common to all these machines are as follows:

- The n registers are referred to as r1 to rn. Typically, access to registers is very fast (relative to the time to access main memory), and $1 \le n \le 32$. However, for the stack machine, $n=0$.

- The main memory consists of m memory locations referred to as locations 0 to $m-1$. Assume that access to memory locations is at least 10 times slower than to registers, so it is worth keeping frequently referenced quantities in registers. Also assume there are enough memory locations to suit any program our compiler will generate.

- There is a set of instructions. To keep the size of our compiler manageable (say one page of Prolog text), the instruction set will not include as many instructions as are found on real computers. More importantly, however, at least one of each major type of instruction is represented, so it is a simple matter to extend the compiler to accommodate more instructions. In addition, labels will be represented as operations, but do not assemble into executable code. The destination of a branch instruction will be denoted as the label identifier.

- There is set of one-bit condition codes. The bits are named N, Z, C, and V. Condition bits are set and cleared by a comparison instruction, and are tested by the branch instructions. The meaning of the bits is the same as for many real computers: N = negative, Z = zero, C = carry, and V = overflow.

9.1   The Register Machine

The instruction set for this machine is as follows:

Operation Code	Name	Description
MOVC x, r	Move Constant	Set register r to the constant x.
MOVM x, r	Move Memory	Set register r to the contents of the memory location x.
STM r, x	Store Memory	Set the contents of memory location x to the contents of register r.
ADD ra, rb	Add	Add the contents of registers ra and rb, setting register rb to the result.

MUL ra, rb	Multiply	Multiply the contents of registers ra and rb, setting register rb to the result.
CMP ra, rb	Compare	Compare the contents of registers ra and rb, setting the condition bits accordingly.
BR x	Branch (unconditional)	Go to the location specified by label x.
BGE x	Branch if Greater than or Equal	If condition bit N equals condition bit V, then go to the location specified by label x.
x:	Label having unique identifier x.	Not a machine instruction. Denotes the destination of a branch.

As an example of the code generator's function, here is an assembly listing resulting from compilation of the factorial program fragment given above into the language required for this machine. Sections of instructions corresponding to source instructions are shown in a box:

```
        MOVC   1, R1      c := 1
        STM    R1, c
        MOVC   1, R1      r := 1
        STM    R1, r
L1:
        MOVM   c, R1
        MOVM   n,R2       If c >= n, go to L2
        CMP    R1,R2
        BGE    L2
        MOVM   c,R1
        MOVC   1,R2       c := c + 1
        ADD    R2, R1
        STM    R1,c
        MOVM   r, R1
        MOVM   c, R2      r := r * c
        MUL    R2, R1
        STM    R1, r
        BR     L1         Go to L1
L2:
```

This may not be the most efficient code possible – for instance, the third instruction could be removed with no effect – but it is easily produced from the code generator described next.

The code generator works by recursive descent of the syntax tree. The predicate cg is defined such that the goal cg(T, R, L) instantiates L to the list of assembly language instructions corresponding to the source program represented by syntax tree T. Variable R is the register containing the result of T. At the leaves of the syntax tree, T will be either an integer or an atom. An integer is moved into register R by means of the MOVC instruction; an atom denotes an address of which the contents are moved into register R by means of the MOVM instruction.

Register rn can be represented by the compound term r(n). Consider the Prolog program:

```
cg(I, R, [rnovc(I,r(R))]) :- integer(I).
cg(A, R, [movm(A,r(R))]) :- atom(A).
cg(X+Y, R, [CX,CY,add(r(RI),r(R))]) :-
                        cg(X, R, CX), R1 is R + 1, cg(Y, R1, CY).
```

The first two clauses deal with the leaves of the syntax tree as indicated above. The third clause deals with the addition of two expressions X and Y. The code generator descends the left-hand argument to generate the code for X affecting register R, returning the list CX. The register number is incremented so that the code for Y will affect the next register. The resulting code is whatever the code for X is, followed by whatever the code for Y is, followed by an ADD instruction that places the sum in register R. This pattern of code generation can be illustrated by the schema:

Code to evaluate X into register r
Code to evaluate Y into register r+1
ADD *r+1, r*

Consider the following example, where we initialise the register number to 1:

```
?- cg(1+2+3, 1, C).
```

c = [[[movc(1, r(1))], [movc(2, r(2))], add(r(2), r(1))],
[movc(3, r(2))], add(r(2) , r(1))]

With minor cosmetic adjustment, the output can be rewritten as:

MOVC	1, R1
MOVC	2, R2
ADD	R2, R1
MOVC	3, R2
ADD	R2, R1

The important point to note is that the code generator has accumulated the sum in R1 so that subsequent additions merely add to R1. Quite different code is generated if we reverse the associativity of the syntax tree:

?- cg(1+(2+3), 1, C).

c =[[movc(1, r(1))], [[movc(2, r(2))], [movc(3, r(3))],
    add(r(3), r(2))], add(r(2), r(1))]

Although this program contains the same number of instructions as the previous program, it uses one more register. This gives a clue as to how we might generate improved code, but we shall not discuss this at the moment.

Another point to note is that the output list is not 'flat'. Its recursive structure actually reflects the structure of the parse tree. As we have seen before, there are three ways to produce a flattened output list. That is, to construct a linearised mapping of the syntax tree: write a program to flatten the list, or create the list by appending the new code to the end of an accumulated list, or create the list by means of difference lists. Adopting the third approach as most sensible, the above program can be rewritten as:

cg(I, R, [movc(I,r(R))|Z]-Z) :- integer(I).
cg(A, R, [movm(A,r(R))|Z]-Z) :- atom(R).
cg(X+Y, R, C0-C2) :-
                    cg(X, R, C0-CI),
                    R1 is R + 1,
                    cg(Y, R1, C1-[add(r(RI),r(R))|C2]).

Now the example goal and answer is:

?- cg(1+2+3, 1, C-[]).

c = [movc(1, r(1)), movc(2, r(2)), add(r(2), r(1)),
    movc(3, r(2)), add(r(2), r(1))]

We may now enrich the program to cope with the factorial example. We need to supply clauses for multiplication, assignment, while, and the sequence operator ';', and for simplicity of explanation we shall not produce a flattened output list. Code for multiplication is generated in the same way as for addition. The assignment node assign(X , Y) causes code to be generated according to this schema:

Code to evaluate Y *into register r*
STM   r, X.

This is possible because it is assumed that X stands for an identifier, and will be used as a label for the memory location containing the value of the identifier.

The sequence operator simply calls the code generator recursively for each argument. The appearance of a while(X, Y) node causes code to be generated according to the schema:

```
Ln:
        Code to test X, branching to Lm if test fails
        Code for Y
        BR Ln
Lm:
```

Another predicate is used for generating the code for tests. The predicate ct is defined such that the goal ct(T, R , C, L) generates code C for syntax tree T affecting register R, including a branch to label L if the code evaluates to a false test.

The following code generator is capable of generating code for the factorial program above, constructing the output unflattened.

```
cg(I, L, [movc(I,r(L))]) :- integer(I).

cg(A, L, [movm(A,r(L))]) :- atom(A).

cg(X+Y, L, [CX,CY,add(r(L1),r(L))]) :-
                cg(X, L, CX),
                L1 is L + 1,
                cg(Y, L1, CY).

cg(X*Y, L, [CX, CY,mul(r(L1),r(L))]) :-
                cg(X, L, CX),
                L1 is L + 1,
                cg(Y, L1, CY).

cg(assign(X,Y), L ,[CY,stm(r(L), X)]) :- cg(Y ,L, CY).

cg(while(X,S), L, [label(R1),CX,SX,br(R1),label(R2)]) :-
                ct(X, L, CX, R2),
                cg(S, L, SX).

cg((A;B), L, [CA,CB]) :- cg(A, L, CA), cg(B, L, CB).

ct(X<Y, L, [CX,CY,cmp(L,L1),bge(R)], R) :-
                cg(X, L, CX),
                L1 is L + 1,
                cg(Y, L1, CY).
```

The source program is stored as a clause:

```
ex((    assign(c,1) ;
```

```
          assign(r,1) ;
          while((c < n), (assign(c, c+1)   ; assign(r, r*c))))).
```

The program can generate code for the factorial example as follows:

```
     ?- ex(X), cg(X, 1, C).
     c =  [[[movc(1,r(1))], stm(r(1),c)],
     [[[movc(1,r(1))], stm(r(1),r)], [label(_61),
     [[movm(c,r(1))], [movm(n, r(1))], cmp(0,1), bge(_64)],
     [[[[movm(c,r(1))], [movc(1,r(2))], add(r(1),r(o))],
     stm(r(1),c)], [[[movm(r,r(1))], [movm(c,r(2))],
     mul(r(2) ,r(1))], stm(r(1),r)]], br(_61), label(_64)]]]
```

Note that the arguments of the label(X) terms are variables. Unique variables are used to name unique labels.

Exercises

1. Rewrite the code generator to construct a flattened output list by means of difference lists.

2. Add clauses to the code generator to compile code for the if...then statement. The compound term if(x, y) can denote the syntax tree node for "if x then y". The term if(x, y, z) can denote "if x then y else z".

9.2   The Single-Accumulator Machine

We shall now consider another hypothetical computer having only one register called the accumulator. As before, instructions and data structures are stored in the main memory, and instructions are executed by the control unit. However, temporary results and constants must be stored in main memory at locations determined during compilation. The instruction set of this machine is shown as follows:

Operation Code	Name	Description
LDA x	Load Accumulator	Set the accumulator to the contents of the memory location x
STA x	Store Accumulator	Set the contents of memory location x to the contents of the accumulator.
ADD x	Add	Add the contents of the memory location referred to by x to the accumulator.
MUL x	Multiply	Multiply the contents of the memory location referred to by x to the accumulator.
CMP x	Compare	Compare the contents of the memory location referred to by x with the accumulator, setting the condition bits accordingly.
BR x	Branch (unconditional)	Go to the location specified by label x.
BGE x	Branch if Greater than or Equal	If condition bit N equals condition bit V, then go to the location specified by label x.
x:	Label having unique identifier x.	Not a machine instruction. Denotes the destination of a branch.

Note that most instructions, even arithmetic operations, access the main memory. As an example of the code generator's function, here is an assembly listing resulting from compilation of the program fragment for factorial given above. It is assumed that the constant 1 is stored in a memory location referred to by the label C1:

LDA	C1	
STA	c	c := 1
LDA	C1	
STA	r	r := 1

L1:

LDA	c	
CMP	n	If c >= n, go to L2
BGE	L2	
LDA	c	
ADD	C1	c := c + 1
STA	c	
LDA	r	
MUL	c	r := r * c
STA	r	
BR	L1	Go to L1

L2:

Again we note that this is not the most efficient program; the third and eighth instructions (not counting labels) could be removed without effect.

Code generation is again by recursive descent, but this time we must take account of having only one register (the accumulator). Before loading the accumulator with a value, it may be necessary to store the accumulator's current contents into a temporary memory location. This was not necessary for the example above, because it was coded by hand. However, consider the arithmetic expression (a+b)*(c+d). The code to evaluate this expression, putting the result in the accumulator, should be

```
LDA    a
ADD    b
STA    T0
LDA    c
ADD    d
MUL    T0
```

Label T0 refers to a memory location for the temporary use of this code. Once the MUL instruction has executed, T0 may be used for another purpose. The general scheme – that the accumulator contents should be stored in a temporary location each time before it is loaded – is too clumsy, as the code for (a + b) shows:

```
LDA       a
STA       T0
LDA       b
ADD       T0
```

In this case, a temporary location is used, yet in fact it is not required at all.

In the code generator that follows, there are three clauses for each operator (where ⊕ stands for an operator): two clauses to handle the special case $x \oplus a$, for expression x and identifier (or constant) a, and a clause for the general case $x \oplus y$, for expressions x and y. The special case $a \oplus x$ is relevant but not considered, because we shall see subsequently that the syntax tree preprocessor will convert all expressions of the form $a \oplus x$ into $x \oplus a$, where ⊕ is a commutative operator.

In the following code generator, the compound term t(n) represents a temporary memory location uniquely identified by n, and c(n) represents a temporary memory location holding the constant n.

```
cg(I, _ ,[lda(c(I))]) :- integer(I).

cg(A, _ ,[lda(A)]) :- atom(A).

cg(X+A, T, [CX, add(A)]) :- atom(A), cg(X, T, CX).

cg(X+I, T, [CX, add(c(I))]) :- integer(I),  cg(X, T, CX).

cg(X+Y, T, [CX, sta(t(T)), CY, add(t(T))]) :-
                    cg(X, T, CX),
                    T1 is  T + 1,
                    cg(Y, T1, CY).

cg(X*A, T, [CX, mul(A)]) :- atom(A),  cg(X, T, CX).

cg(X*I, T, [CX, mul(c(I))]) :- integer(I),  cg(X, T, CX).

cg(X*Y, T, [CX, sta(t(T)), CY, mul(t(T))]) :-
                    cg(X, T, CX),
                    T1 is T + 1,
                    cg(Y, T1, CY).

cg(while(X, S), T, [label(L1), CX, SX, br(L1), label(L2)]) :-
                    ct(X, T, CX, L2),
                    cg(S, T, SX).

cg((A; B), T, [CA, CB]) :- cg(A, T, CA), cg(B, T, CB).

cg(assign(A, X), T, [CX,sta(A)])  :-  cg(X, T, CX).

ct(X<A, T, [CX, cmp(A), bge(R)], R) :- atom(A),  cg(X, T, CX).
```

```
ct(X<Y, T ,[CY, sta(t(T)), CX, cmp(t(T)), bge(L)], L) :-
                 cg(Y, T, CY),
                 T1 is T + 1,
                 cg(X, T1, CX).
```

This code generator also has the satisfying property that left-associative operations are accumulated: the expression (a + b + c + d) generates

```
LDA     a
ADD     b
ADD     c
ADD     d
```

On the other hand, note that the expression (a + (b + (c + d))) generates

```
LDA     a
STA     T0
LDA     b
STA     T1
LDA     c
ADD     d
ADD     T1
ADD     T0
```

Thus we see that temporary locations are allocated in the same general way as registers are allocated by the code generator for the register machine. The result of running the code generator on the factorial program fragment (using procedure ex from the previous program) is:

```
?- ex(X),  cg(X, 1, Q).
```

*Q = [[(lda(c(1)))], sta(c)], [[[lda(c(1))],sta(r)],
[label(_57), [[lda(c)], cmp(n), bge(_60)],
[[[[lda(c)], add(c(1))], sta(c)], [[[lda(r)],
mul(c)], sta(r)]], br(_57), label(_60)]*

Again the output has not been flattened, and unique variables are used to denote unique labels.

Exercises

1. Rewrite the code generator to construct a flattened output list by means of difference lists.

2. Add clauses to the code generator to compile code for the if...then statement. The compound term if(x, y) can denote the syntax tree node for "if x then y". The term if(x, y, z) can denote "if x then y else z".

9.3   The Stack Machine

We shall now consider the stack machine, which has no registers or condition codes at all. The control unit accesses a first-in-last-out stack. When an expression is evaluated, arguments are pushed onto the stack, and operations pop arguments from the stack and push their result onto the stack. Thus, temporary results and constants are all stored implicitly on the stack. In principle, the control unit need access only the top element of the stack. The instruction set of our hypothetical stack machine is shown as follows:

Operation Code	Name	Description
PUSH x	Push	Push the contents of the memory location referred to by address x onto the stack.
PUSHC i	Push Constant	Push the constant i onto the stack.
POP x	Pop	Pop the top element of the stack, moving it to the memory location referred to by x.
ADD	Add	Pop the top two elements from the stack, add them, and push the sum onto the stack.
MUL	Multiply	Pop the top two elements from the stack, multiply them, and push the sum onto the stack.
CLT	Compare Less Than	Pop the top element from the stack. If it is greater than the new top of stack, then pop the stack and push 1, else pop the stack and push 0.
BR x	Branch (unconditional)	Go to the location specified by label x.
BZ x	Branch if Zero	Pop the top element from the stack. If it is zero, then branch to the location specified by x.
x:	Label having unique identifier x.	Not a machine instruction. Denotes the destination of a branch.

As an example of the code generator's function, here is an assembly listing resulting from compiling the factorial program fragment given above:

above:

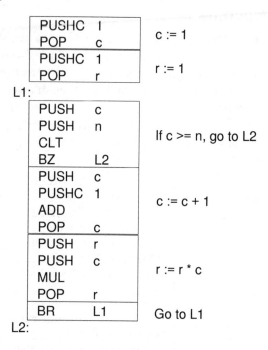

The code generator for the stack machine is perhaps the easiest to write, as there is no need to maintain registers and temporary locations. Thus, the cg predicate need not have any arguments in addition to the parse tree input and the assembly list output. Again recursive descent is used. When a leaf of the syntax tree is encountered, code is generated to push the leaf value onto the stack. Nodes of the syntax tree refer to operations on the contents of the stack. Note that the comparison operator is treated just as any other operator, so a separate ct procedure is not needed.

```
cg(I, pushc(I)) :- integer(I).
cg(A, [push(A)]) :- atom(A).
cg(X+Y, [CX,CY,add]) :- cg(X,CX), cg(Y,CY).
cg(X*Y, [CX,CY,mul]) :- cg(X,CX), cg(Y,CY).
cg(X<Y, [CX,CY,clt]) :- cg(X,CX), cg(Y,CY).
cg(assign(X,Y), [CY,pop(X)]) :- cg(Y,CY).
cg(while(X,S), [label(R1),CX,bz(R2),SX,br(R1),label(R2)])
                :- cg(X,CX), cg(S,SX).
```

cg((A;B), [CA,CB]) :- cg(A,CA), cg(B,CB).

Consider now the effect of accumulating left-associative expressions: the expression (a + b + c + d) generates

```
PUSH    a
PUSH    b
ADD
PUSH    c
ADD
PUSH    d
ADD
```

but the expression (a + (b + (c + d))) generates

```
PUSH    a
PUSH    b
PUSH    c
PUSH    d
ADD
ADD
ADD
```

This time the effect of right-associative operations is to increase the amount of stack used as temporary memory. The result of running the code generator on the factorial program fragment is:

```
?- ex(X),  cg(X,Y).
    v = [[pushc(1), pop(c)], [[pushc(1), pop(r)],
    [label(_56), [[push(c)], [push(n)], clt],
    bz(_58), [[[[push(c)], pushc(1), add], pop(c)],
    [[[push(r)], [push(c)], mul], pop(r)]], br(_56),
    label(_58)]]]
```

Exercises

1. Rewrite the code generator to construct a flattened output list by means of difference lists.
2. Add clauses to the code generator to compile code for the if...then statement. The compound term if(x, y) can denote the syntax tree node for "if x then y". The term if(x, y, z) can denote "if x then y else z".

9.4   Optimisation: Preprocessing the Syntax Tree

The various optimisations discussed in this section are all accomplished by rewriting the syntax tree before it is given to the code generator. Three preprocessing steps will be introduced: tree rotation, constant folding, and strength reduction.

Tree Rotation

In all the recursive descent algorithms given above, we have seen that for a commutative operator $\oplus$, fewer resources (registers, memory locations, stack depth) are needed for expressions of the form $x \oplus a$ (for expression x and identifier (or constant) a). This suggests a possible preprocessing of the syntax tree, whereby all nodes of the form $a \oplus x$ are simply 'rotated' into the form $x \oplus a$ before code is generated from it.

Such preprocessing can also be done by recursive descent. The predicate rot is defined such that the goal rot(X, Y) transforms syntax tree X into syntax tree Y, where all commutative operations over a constant a and an expression x are written in the form $x \oplus a$.

    rot(X, X) :- atomic(X).
    rot(X+Y, Y1+X) :- atomic(X), rot(Y, Y1).
    rot(X+Y, X1+Y1) :- rot(X, X1),   rot(Y, Y1).
    rot(X*Y, Y1*X) :- atomic(X),   rot(Y, Y1).
    rot(X*Y, X1*Y1) :- rot(X, X1),   rot(Y, Y1).

Leaves of the syntax tree are handled by the first clause. The remaining clauses handle addition and multiplication. Other operations can be accommodated, for example to add a clause to transform expressions of the form $a{-}x$ to $x{+}\,({-}a)$.

The general case of this transformation is more interesting. Suppose x and y are expressions, and that x is more deeply nested than y. It is sensible in this case to transform the expression $x \oplus y$ into $y \oplus x$ before generating instructions. Although x is not a constant, it is still the case that fewer resources will be required for computing $y \oplus x$, and the program given above will not detect this. The next program does.

Predicate rot is defined such that the goal rot(X, Y, W) transforms syntax tree X into syntax tree Y of depth W, where nodes of the form $x \oplus y$ are rotated so that y is less deeply nested than x. The predicate swop is used to establish the order in which operands are assigned to a node of the transformed syntax tree. Suppose X and Y are expressions, and Wx and Wy are their depths. The goal swop(Wx, Wy, X, Y, R, L, W) will instantiate R to the expression that should appear on the right-hand side of an operator, and L to the expression that should appear on the left-hand side of an operator, and W to the depth of the deeper of the two expressions.

```
rot(X, X, 0) :- atomic(X).

rot(X+Y, A+B, W) :-
        rot(X, X1, Wx),
        rot(Y, Y1, Wy),
        swop(Wx, Wy, X1, Y1, A, B, W).

rot(X*Y, A*B, W) :-
        rot(X, X1, Wx),
        rot(Y, Y1, Wy),
        swop(Wx, Wy, X1, Y1, A, B, W).

swop(Wx, Wy, X, Y, X, Y, Wx) :- Wx > Wy, !.
swop(Wx, Wy, X, Y, Y, X, Wy) :- Wy > Wx, !.
swop(W, W, X, Y, X, Y, N) :- N is W + 1.
```

Constant Folding

Another preprocessing step to consider is the evaluation of constant expressions. For example, the expression 2+3+a will generate more efficient code if it is first transformed to 5+a. This is a simple case, where the two constants to be added are direct leaves of the addition node. The following program works by recursive descent. The predicate fold is defined such that the goal fold(X, Y) transforms expression X to expression Y, where Y contains no operator for which both operands are constants.

```
fold(X,X) :- atomic(X).
fold(X+Y, Z) :- fold(X, X1), fold(Y, Y1), operate(X1+Y1, Z).
foid(X*Y, Z) :- fold(X, X1), fold(Y, Y1), operate(X1*Y1, Z).

operate(X+Y, Z) :- integer(X), integer(Y), Z is X + Y.
operate(X*Y, Z) :- integer(X), integer(Y), Z is X * Y.
operate(X, X).
```

In most situations, further processing is required to expose constant expressions. For example, the expression 2+a+3 will not be modified by the above program, as the 2 and 3 are not direct leaves of the same '+' node. Also, for the expression 21*(a+5) to be handled by the above program, it is first necessary to transform the expression to the equivalent (21*a) + (21*5). Many common cases can be handled by simply adding extra clauses to fold, for example fold(C*(X+Y), Z) :- integer(C), fold((C*X)+(C*Y), Z).

Strength Reduction

The final preprocessing step we shall consider is strength reduction. Many operations have identities: $a+0 = a$; $a*1 = a$, and so forth. For machines containing a 'shift' instruction in their instruction set, multiplication (or division) of the positive integer a by the constant 2^n can be compiled by shifting a left (or right) by n bits. We shall introduce a new syntax tree node shift(x,n) to represent the operation of shifting the value of expression x left by n bits. Also, for machines containing an increment instruction in their instruction set, addition by the constant 1 can be compiled efficiently. We shall introduce a new syntax tree node inc(x) to represent the operation of adding 1 to the value of expression x.

The predicate reduce is defined such that the goal reduce(X, Y) transforms expression X into the strength-reduced equivalent expression Y. The predicate power2 is simply a table of some (not carefully selected) integer powers of 2, so that power2(x, y) is true for some $x = 2^y$.

```
reduce(X+0, Y) :- reduce(X, Y).
reduce(X+1, inc(Y)) :- reduce(X, Y).
reduce(X*1, Y) :- reduce(X, Y).
reduce(X*0, 0).
reduce(X*C, shift(Y,N)) :- power2(C, N), reduce(X, Y).

power2(2, 1.)
power2(4, 2).
power2(8, 3).
power2(256, 8).
power2(16777216, 24).
```

In a real program you would need to provide a more complete power2 predicate. Again note that we are assuming that the commutative nodes have been rotated into the form $x \oplus c$ (for constant c). The inclusion of a clause such as

```
reduce(X+X, Y) :- reduce(X*2, Y).
```

can help to handle common subexpressions efficiently, but requires careful consideration of the instruction set of the target machine. To generate code from trees containing shift and inc nodes, it is necessary to add clauses to the code generators discussed above.

9.5   Peephole Optimisation

Optimisations can be applied even after a code sequence has been generated. The purpose of peephole optimisation is to transform stereo-typical code sequences into more efficient ones. For example, the stack machine code sequence

```
    ⋮
PUSHC   0
BZ      L1
    ⋮
```

can be improved by removing the PUSHC instruction and changing the BZ to a BR. It is called peephole optimisation because we are interested in looking only at patterns that are two or three instructions long. Peephole optimisation can be applicable for two reasons: the simple recursive descent of the code generator does not use sufficient con-textual information to generate sophisticated code, and the target machine may contain special-purpose instructions that can replace commonly generated sequences of instructions. An example of the latter case is when the machine contains an instruction to set a register or memory location to zero (it is usually called the 'clear' instruction). Thus for the stack machine, the sequence

```
    ⋮
PUSHC   0
POP     A
    ⋮
```

can be transformed into the sequence

```
    ⋮
CLR     A
    ⋮
```

provided that the machine has a CLR instruction. It is possible to represent this transformation as a strength reduction, to be implement-ed by adding a new parse tree node clear(x) and adding the clause

reduce(assign(X,0), clear(X)).

It is then necessary to add a clause to the code generator to handle the clear node. An alternative is to postprocess the generated code.

What follows is a *peephole optimiser* that will transform a list of assembly instructions (as Prolog terms) into a possibly more efficient list of instructions. The predicate peep is defined such that the goal peep(X, Y) transforms a list X of instructions into a possibly improved

list Y. Predicate idiom is a table of possible code idioms (in this example
we shall use stack machine instructions) defined such that the goal
idiom(X, Y) succeeds if X can be replaced by Y.

```
peep(X, Y) :- idiom(X, I), peep(I, Y).
peep(X, X).
```

```
idiom([br(L), label(L)|Z], [label(L)|Z]).
Idiom([pushc(0), bz(L)|Z], [br(L)|Z]).
idiom([H|T], [H|Z]) :- idiom(T, Z).
```

Two idioms are given as examples: branching to the next instruction
and conditionally branching on zero. In the case of branching to the
next instruction, the action of the optimiser is simply to remove the
branch instruction. In the case of conditionally branching given an
argument of zero, the action is again to remove the branch instruction.

More idioms are easily accommodated by adding more clauses before
the last clause. This peephole optimiser has the useful property that
transformations introduced by the optimiser are themselves subjected
to optimisation in the context where they are placed.

Predicate idiom fails if no idiom can be found. The second clause of
peep represents the identity transformation in case no idioms are
found.

Bibliographic Notes

This chapter was inspired by David H.D. Warren's paper 'Logic programming and compiler writing', *Software: Practice and Experience* **10**,
97-125, 1980. Standard compiler writing techniques can be found in
Principles of Compiler Design, by Aho, A.V. and Ullman, J.D. (Addison-
Wesley, 1977).

The clever way to arrange peephole optimisations is due to my
colleague Chris Mellish.

CHAPTER TEN
CASE STUDY: THE FAST FOURIER
TRANSFORM IN PROLOG

10.1 Introduction

It is not widely appreciated that Prolog has a role to play in the development of numerical methods. As an example of an unexpected but satisfying application of Prolog, this case study will demonstrate how Prolog can be used to derive a formulation of the Fast Fourier Transform.

An n-point Discrete Fourier Transform algorithm has a rather elegant formulation as follows. Let $p(x)$ be a polynomial in x of degree $n-1$, where n is 2^m for some m (in other words, where n is a power of 2):

$$p(x) = a_0 + a_1 x + a_2 x^2 + \ldots + a_{n-1} x^{n-1}.$$

We are interested in evaluating this polynomial at powers of the nth roots of unity. An nth root of unity ω^k is a complex constant that satisfies $\omega^k = \exp(2\pi i \, k/n)$. When nth roots of unity are plotted on the complex plane, they form the vertices of a regular n-gon inscribed on the unit circle, with ω^0 at point $(1,0)$. For example, the eight powers of the eighth roots of unity are plotted as follows:

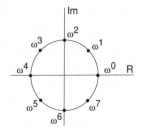

To calculate an n-point (or order-n) Discrete Fourier Transform (DFT), simply use the n coefficients as inputs, and the outputs will be the value of the order $n-1$ polynomial evaluated at the n powers of the nth roots of unity. For example, here is a diagram showing the inputs and outputs for a DFT of order 8:

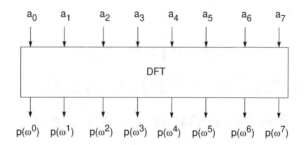

Because there are n polynomials each having n products, the computational complexity of the DFT is about $O(n^2)$. In principle, because the problem has a certain structure (explained below), a complexity of $O(n \log_2 n)$ should be possible. The Fast Fourier Transform (FFT) is an algorithm that achieves this efficiency by a clever method involving systematic rearrangement of partial results usually called 'shuffling' or 'bit reversal'. Practical algorithms for the FFT have been well known since the early 1960s. These are written in imperative languages such as FORTRAN or C, and cannot be translated directly into Prolog because they make use of updatable arrays. Even if we used a package for implementing updatable arrays in Prolog, the resulting program would be unsatisfactory because instead of exploiting the Prolog idiom, we are simply writing a C program in Prolog. The result is invariably a bad program. A better way to begin is to see whether there is an approach to the problem that is idiomatic to Prolog.

In this chapter we shall show how the FFT may be automatically derived. To do this, we perform abstract interpretation of the polynomials, and convert them into dataflow graphs that share common subexpressions. The result is a dataflow graph that demonstrates an explicit reason why FFT is 'fast'. This graph represents a set of expressions that can be solved, if necessary, for specific values of the coefficients, using any suitable language for numerical calculation.

10.2 Notation for Polynomials

We may write the polynomial $p(x)$ of degree $n-1$ in the following indexed form, where the $i_0, i_1, ..., i_{n-1}$ are called indices:

$$p_{[i_0, i_1, ..., i_{n-1}]}(x) = a_{i_0} + a_{i_1} x + a_{i_2} x^2 + ... + a_{i_{n-1}} x^{n-1}$$

For example,

$$p_{[1,3,5,7]}(x) = a_1 + a_3 x + a_5 x^2 + a_7 x^3.$$

This notation permits the definition of polynomials with different arrangements of the coefficients with the powers of x. This notation has a practical benefit that will become obvious later when describing the clausal formulation.

10.3 The DFT

Letting ω^k denote the kth power of the nth root of unity, we wish to compute all the $p(\omega^0), p(\omega^1), ..., p(\omega^{n-1})$. The computation of a $p(\omega^k)$ proceeds by recursively decomposing a given polynomial into the sum of two polynomials according to the Danielson–Lanczos lemma:

$$p_{[i_0,i_1,...,i_{n-1}]}(\omega^k) = p_{[i_0,i_2,...,i_{n-2}]}(\omega^{2k}) + p_{[i_1,i_3,...,i_{n-1}]}(\omega^{2k}).$$

Note that this amounts to recursively rewriting a polynomial having n indices into two polynomials each having the $n/2$ alternating indices of the original polynomial. The recursion terminates when only one index is encountered, in which case we rewrite this as an expression consisting of the index coefficient: $p_{[i]}(\omega^k) = a_i$.

10.4 Example: 8-point DFT

For practice, let's go through the complete recursive evaluation of the polynomial for an 8-point DFT. Let $p(x)$ be a polynomial of degree 7 in x:

$$p(x)_{[0,1,2,3,4,5,6,7]} = a_0 + a_1 x + a_2 x^2 + a_3 x^3 + a_4 x^4 + a_5 x^5 + a_6 x^6 + a_7 x^7.$$

According to the Danielson–Lanczos lemma, $p(x)$ can be rewritten in our 'index' notation as

$$p(x) = p_{[0,2,4,6]}(x^2) + x p_{[1,3,5,7]}(x^2)$$

where

$$p_{[0,2,4,6]}(x) = a_0 + a_2 x + a_4 x^2 + a_6 x^3$$
$$p_{[1,3,5,7]}(x) = a_1 + a_3 x + a_5 x^2 + a_7 x^3$$

Letting ω^k denote the kth power of the eighth root of unity, we wish to compute the following: $p(\omega^0), p(\omega^1), ..., p(\omega^7)$.

Now rewrite each polynomial in ω^k according to the above scheme. Remember that powers of the nth roots of unity are all written modulo n (here n=8), so $(\omega^6)^2 = \omega^4$. Also, for convenience, we will not use the 'sign' identities $\omega^4 = -\omega^0$, $\omega^5 = -\omega^1$, and so forth:

$$p(\omega^0) = p_{[0,2,4,6]}(\omega^0) + \omega^0 \, p_{[1,3,5,7]}(\omega^0)$$
$$p(\omega^1) = p_{[0,2,4,6]}(\omega^2) + \omega^1 \, p_{[1,3,5,7]}(\omega^2)$$
$$p(\omega^2) = p_{[0,2,4,6]}(\omega^4) + \omega^2 \, p_{[1,3,5,7]}(\omega^4)$$
$$p(\omega^3) = p_{[0,2,4,6]}(\omega^6) + \omega^3 \, p_{[1,3,5,7]}(\omega^6)$$
$$p(\omega^4) = p_{[0,2,4,6]}(\omega^0) + \omega^4 \, p_{[1,3,5,7]}(\omega^0)$$
$$p(\omega^5) = p_{[0,2,4,6]}(\omega^2) + \omega^5 \, p_{[1,3,5,7]}(\omega^2)$$
$$p(\omega^6) = p_{[0,2,4,6]}(\omega^4) + \omega^6 \, p_{[1,3,5,7]}(\omega^4)$$
$$p(\omega^7) = p_{[0,2,4,6]}(\omega^6) + \omega^7 \, p_{[1,3,5,7]}(\omega^6)$$

Proceeding with the next level of recursion, we need to find

$$p_{[0,2,4,6]}(\omega^0) = p_{[0,4]}(\omega^0) + \omega^0 \, p_{[2,6]}(\omega^0)$$
$$p_{[0,2,4,6]}(\omega^2) = p_{[0,4]}(\omega^4) + \omega^2 \, p_{[2,6]}(\omega^4)$$
$$p_{[0,2,4,6]}(\omega^4) = p_{[0,4]}(\omega^0) + \omega^4 \, p_{[2,6]}(\omega^0)$$
$$p_{[0,2,4,6]}(\omega^6) = p_{[0,4]}(\omega^4) + \omega^6 \, p_{[2,6]}(\omega^4)$$

and

$$p_{[1,3,5,7]}(\omega^0) = p_{[1,5]}(\omega^0) + \omega^0 \, p_{[3,7]}(\omega^0)$$
$$p_{[1,3,5,7]}(\omega^2) = p_{[1,5]}(\omega^4) + \omega^2 \, p_{[3,7]}(\omega^4)$$
$$p_{[1,3,5,7]}(\omega^4) = p_{[1,5]}(\omega^0) + \omega^4 \, p_{[3,7]}(\omega^0)$$
$$p_{[1,3,5,7]}(\omega^6) = p_{[1,5]}(\omega^4) + \omega^6 \, p_{[3,7]}(\omega^4)$$

Finally, the 2-index polynomials can be reduced immediately to:

$$p_{[0,4]}(\omega^0) = a_0 + \omega^0 \, a_4$$
$$p_{[0,4]}(\omega^4) = a_0 + \omega^4 \, a_4$$
$$p_{[2,6]}(\omega^0) = a_2 + \omega^0 \, a_6$$
$$p_{[2,6]}(\omega^4) = a_2 + \omega^4 \, a_6$$
$$p_{[1,5]}(\omega^0) = a_1 + \omega^0 \, a_5$$
$$p_{[1,5]}(\omega^4) = a_1 + \omega^4 \, a_5$$
$$p_{[3,7]}(\omega^0) = a_3 + \omega^0 \, a_7$$
$$p_{[3,7]}(\omega^4) = a_3 + \omega^4 \, a_7$$

So now each polynomial in a power of a root of unity has been reduced to a sum of products of coefficients and complex constants. For example, tracing back through the recursion, we can reconstruct the following expression for $p(\omega^6)$:

$$p(\omega^6) = a_0 + \omega^0 a_4 + \omega^4 \left(a_2 + \omega^0 a_6 \right) + a_1 + \omega^0 a_5 + \omega^4 \left(a_3 + \omega^0 a_7 \right)$$

This is a sum-of-products expression in containing only coefficients (used as the inputs) and complex constants.

10.5 Naive Implementation of the DFT

Now we can do this in Prolog. We write a root of unity raised to the power k as the compound term w^k, using the infix operator '^'. We can write the polynomial $p_{[i_0,i_1,\ldots,i_{n-1}]}(\omega^k)$ as the compound term

   p([$i_0, i_1, \ldots, i_{n-1}$], w^k)

so for example we can write the polynomial p([0,2,4,6], w^6). We can write coefficients as a compound term with functor a, for example, a(3).

As each recursive call requires the odd and even indices, we first define the predicate alternate, such that the goal alternate(L,L1,L2) succeeds when L1 is the list of odd elements of L, and L2 is the set of even elements of L. Remember, by 'odd' we mean the 'odd-sequenced' element of the list (i.e., the first, the third, the fifth element, etc.), and *not* the elements that are 'odd numbers'.

The procedure consists of the following two clauses:

   alternate([],[],[]).
   alternate([A,B|T], [A|T1], [B|T2]) :- alternate(T, T1, T2).

By inspection of their heads, these clauses are mutually exclusive, and so as we might expect, alternate is deterministic.

Finally, we define the predicate eval, for evaluating a polynomial for a given argument. However, the result will not be a calculation, but instead will be an abstract interpretation. That is, the result of eval will be a sum-of-products *expression* consisting only of coefficients and complex constants. When used to find N-point DFTs, goal eval(P,X,N) succeeds when X is the expression which specifies the evaluation of polynomial P as a complex root of unity. The eval procedure consists of the following two goals, which reflect the base case and the recursive case of the Danielson–Lanczos lemma given earlier:

   eval(p([I],V), a(I), _).

   eval(p([L,V^P), A1+V^P*A2, N) :-
                    alternate(L, L1, L2),
                    P1 is (P*2) mod N,
                    eval(p(L1,V^P1), A1, N),
                    eval(p(L2,V^P1), A2, N).

The first clause specifies the base case for the recursion. The second clause is the recursive case, which composes the sum-and-product term (in its second argument), finds the alternating indices, multiplies the power (ensuring it is modulo N), and recurs on the two decomposed polynomials. The two clauses are mutually exclusive (the alternate goal fails if its first agument is a one-element list), and so eval is deterministic.

As an example, the following goal evaluates the input polynomial at an 8th root of unity w^6, which is one of the eight goals required for an 8-point DFT:

?- eval(p([0,1,2,3,4,5,6,7], w^6, X, 8).

$$X = a(0)+w^0{*}a(4)+w^4{*}(a(2)+w^0{*}a(6))$$
$$+w^6{*}(a(1)+w^0{*}a(5)+w^4{*}(a(3)+w^0{*}a(7)))$$

Each w^k is a complex constant, and it is a straightforward task to convert the above expression for X to a piece of code in an imperative program. However, to compute an n-point DFT, an eval goal must be satisfied at each of the n powers of the n roots of unity, like this:

?- eval(p([0,1,2,3,4,5,6,7], w^0), X0, 8),
    eval(p([0,1,2,3,4,5,6,7], w^1), X1, 8),
    eval(p([0,1,2,3,4,5,6,7], w^2), X2, 8),
    eval(p([0,1,2,3,4,5,6,7], w^3), X3, 8),
    eval(p([0,1,2,3,4,5,6,7], w^4), X4, 8),
    eval(p([0,1,2,3,4,5,6,7], w^5), X5, 8),
    eval(p([0,1,2,3,4,5,6,7], w^6), X6, 8),
    eval(p([0,1,2,3,4,5,6,7], w^7), X7, 8).

Notice the regularity and common subexpressions in the resulting evaluations:

$X0 = a(0)+w^0{*}a(4)+w^0{*}(a(2)+w^0{*}a(6))+w^0{*}(a(1)+w^0{*}a(5)+w^0{*}(a(3)+w^0{*}a(7)))$

$X1 = a(0)+w^4{*}a(4)+w^2{*}(a(2)+w^4{*}a(6))+w^1{*}(a(1)+w^4{*}a(5)+w^2{*}(a(3)+w^4{*}a(7)))$

$X2 = a(0)+w^0{*}a(4)+w^4{*}(a(2)+w^0{*}a(6))+w^2{*}(a(1)+w^0{*}a(5)+w^4{*}(a(3)+w^0{*}a(7)))$

$X3 = a(0)+w^4{*}a(4)+w^6{*}(a(2)+w^4{*}a(6))+w^3{*}(a(1)+w^4{*}a(5)+w^6{*}(a(3)+w^4{*}a(7)))$

$X4 = a(0)+w^0{*}a(4)+w^0{*}(a(2)+w^0{*}a(6))+w^4{*}(a(1)+w^0{*}a(5)+w^0{*}(a(3)+w^0{*}a(7)))$

$X5 = a(0)+w^4{*}a(4)+w^2{*}(a(2)+w^4{*}a(6))+w^5{*}(a(1)+w^4{*}a(5)+w^2{*}(a(3)+w^4{*}a(7)))$

$X6 = a(0)+w^0{*}a(4)+w^4{*}(a(2)+w^0{*}a(6))+w^6{*}(a(1)+w^0{*}a(5)+w^4{*}(a(3)+w^0{*}a(7)))$

$X7 = a(0)+w^4{*}a(4)+w^6{*}(a(2)+w^4{*}a(6))+w^7{*}(a(1)+w^4{*}a(5)+w^6{*}(a(3)+w^4{*}a(7)))$

This suggests there is much to be gained by exploiting common subexpressions when one needs to calculate the values for X0 to X7.

10.6 From DFT to FFT

The key to the *Fast* Fourier Transform (FFT) is the saving of work by computing identical subexpressions once only. Conventional algorithms for the FFT are greatly complicated by the need to deal with these identical subexpressions. Typically, the common subexpressions are computed first, and assigned to certain elements of an array from where they are accessed later. The method for arranging the right pattern of storage and retrieval is known as shuffling or bit reversal. This requires the rearrangement of entries in an array according to a systematic procedure. Because this assumes the existence of mutable arrays, standard technique is entirely alien to the world of logic programming. Because the eight eval goals required for an 8-point FFT are independent, and because the clausal formulation abstracts away from notations of data storage, the *raison d'être* of the FFT is not met by the eval predicate alone.

We shall now describe a way to formulate the FFT which works by merging common subexpressions wherever they may be found in the input. We shall see that this is enough to obtain the effect of the FFT without sacrificing the elegance of the original specification in terms of the eval predicate.

10.7 Merging Common Subexpressions

Suppose we are given the two expressions

$$a+b*c \; ; \; d+b*c$$

which have the following trees:

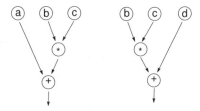

The product b*c is common to both, so it can be computed once and the result sent to both sums, as shown in the following dataflow graph:

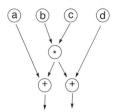

Constructing such a directed acyclic graph (or DAG) for merging common subexpressions is a fairly common operation done by optimising compilers. Here we shall use it to synthesise a new formulation of the FFT.

We need to rewrite algebraic expressions as dataflow graphs. The dataflow graphs will be constructed so as to fold common subexpressions, that is, dataflow graphs will be DAGs. A dataflow graph will be represented by a list of nodes. A node is represented by the binary term n(*n1*, *t*), where *n1* is a unique node identifier which is used to name the output of the node, and *t* is a term which is either

- a compound term representing a constant, possibly a complex constant such as w^6, or a subscripted parameter such as a(1);
- a compound term of the form op(*p*, *n2*, *n3*), representing an arithmetic operation, where *p* describes a computation performed by the node, and *n2* and *n3* are the identifiers of the nodes that compute the arguments for node *n1*.

For example, the expression 17+a is represented by the following graph (node numbers are shown in the upper left-hand corner of the node):

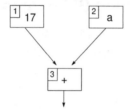

which is represented as the list [n(1,17), n(2,a), n(3,op(+,1,2))].

The merging of common subexpressions can be depicted as follows. The expression (a+b)*(a+b), which has the graph

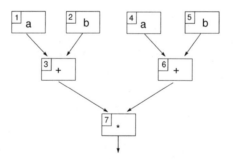

and represented by the list

$$[n(1,a), n(2,b), n(3,op(+,1,2)), n(4,a),$$
$$n(5,b), n(6, op(+,4,5)), n(7, op(*,3,6))]$$

can be folded into the DAG

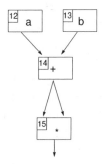

which itself is represented as the list

[n(12,a), n(13(b), n(14,op(+,12,13)), n(15, op(*,14,14))].

10.8 The Graph Generator

The purpose of the graph generator is to construct a DAG from an input expression. The DAG is constructed in such as way that all common subexpressions will be merged. The graph generator is a simplified (and much more elegant) version of the usual algorithm for constructing directed acyclic graphs. The generator consists of three procedures. The predicate gen succeeds for goal gen(e, *d*, *v*), where *e* is the input expression, the output list of nodes is represented by the difference list *d* which will be written in *front–back* form; and *v* is an accumulator used to generate unique node numbers. The procedure is written with one clause for each operator that might be encountered in the input expression. The operator ';' is used to separate multiple expressions, and we shall see later how this is used in the FFT.

The program works by descending the expression tree, and for each operation or operand, produces one node. It then checks to see whether the node may be introduced into the output list.

```
/* gen(InTree, ListOutFront-ListOutBack, NodeIndex) */

gen(X+Y, L0-L3, A) :- !,
        gen(X, L0-L1, A1),
        gen(Y, L1-L2, A2),
        node(n(A, op(+,A1,A2), L2-L3).

gen(X*Y, L0-L3, A) :- !,
        gen(X, L0-L1, A1),
        gen(Y, L1-L2, A2),
        node(n(A, op(*,A1,A2)), L2-L3).

gen((X;Y), L0-L2, _) :- !, gen(X, L0-L1, _), gen(Y, L1-L2, _).
```

```
gen(X, L0-L1, A) :- node(n(A,X), L0-L1).
```

Notice that only clauses for addition, multiplication, sequence and constant are given. It is straightforward to add clauses to generate graph nodes for other operations.

The next procedure is named node. Predicate node succeeds if for goal node(n, d), n is a computation node encountered in the input expression, and the current list of nodes is represented by the difference list d which will be written in *front–back* form. Goal node(N,F,B) just checks whether the node N generated by gen is suitable to be included in the difference list D. There are three cases:

- The first node is always in the list.
- Or, the node may not be added if it does the same thing as a node already in the list.
- Otherwise, add a new node with an incremented node number.

The code for node is deceptively simple, and repays close study:

```
/* node(TryNode, OutDiffList) */

node(n(1,N), []-[n(1,N)]) :- !.
node(N, L-L) :- find(N,L), !.
node(n(A1,N1), [n(A,N)|T]-[n(A1,N1),n(A,N)|T]) :- A1 is A + 1.
```

Notice that not only does A1 name the new node, but it is passed back (through the first argument of node) so that gen can know the latest node number.

Finally, the procedure find, which is called by node to check whether a node already exists in the DAG under construction, is just a deterministic check for membership of a list:

```
/* find(Element, List) */

find([X, [X|_]) :- !.
find(X, [_|T],) :- find(X, T).
```

10.9 Example Run: 8-point FFT

With gen and eval as defined previously, and assuming the declaration of the infix operator '^', we can pose the following query:

```
?-  eval(p([0,1,2,3,4,5,6,7], w^0), X0, 8),
    eval(p([0,1,2,3,4,5,6,7], w^1), X1, 8),
    eval(p([0,1,2,3,4,5,6,7], w^2), X2, 8),
    eval(p([0,1,2,3,4,5,6,7], w^3), X3, 8),
    eval(p([0,1,2,3,4,5,6,7], w^4), X4, 8),
    eval(p([0,1,2,3,4,5,6,7], w^5), X5, 8),
```

```
eval(p([0,1,2,3,4,5,6,7], w^6), X6, 8),
eval(p([0,1,2,3,4,5,6,7], w^7), X7, 8),
gen((X0;X1;X2;X3;X4;X5;X6;X7), []-L, _).
```

Ignoring the X terms (whose values we have seen above), the following graph (in list representation) is found:

L = [n(64,op(+,49,63)), n(63,op(*,62,52)), n(62,w^7),
n(61,op(+,42,60)), n(60,op(*,47,44)), n(59,op(+,31,58)),
n(58,op(*,57,38)), n(57,w^5), n(56,op(+,11,55)), n(55,op(*,24,21)),
n(54,op(+,49,53)), n(53,op(*,50,52)), n(52,op(+,34,51)),
n(51,op(*,47,36)), n(50,w^3), n(49,op(+,26,48)), n(48,op(*,47,29)),
n(47,w^6), n(46,op(+,42,45)), n(45,op(*,27,44)), n(44,op(+,15,43)),
n(43,op(*,24,19)), n(42,op(+,5,41)), n(41,op(*,24,9)),
n(40,op(+,31,39)), n(39,op(*,32,38)), n(38,op(+,34,37)),
n(37,op(*,27,36)), n(36,op(+,16,35)), n(35,op(*,24,17)),
n(34,op(+,12,33)), n(33,op(*,24,13)), n(32,w^1), n(31,op(+,26,30)),
n(30,op(*,27,29)), n(29,op(+,6,28)), n(28,op(*,24,7)), n(27,w^2),
n(26,op(+,1,25)), n(25,op(*,24,3)), n(24,w^4), n(23,op(+,11,22)),
n(22,op(*,2,21)), n(21,op(+,15,20)), n(20,op(*,2,19)),
n(19,op(+,16,18)), n(18,op(*,2,17)), n(17,a(7)), n(16,a(3)),
n(15,op(+,12,14)), n(14,op(*,2,13)), n(13,a(5)), n(12,a(1)),
n(11,op(+,5,10)), n(10,op(*,2,9)), n(9,op(+,6,8)), n(8,op(*,2,7)),
n(7,a(6)), n(6,a(2)), n(5,op(+,1,4)), n(4,op(*,2,3)), n(3,a(4)), n(2,w^0),
n(1,a(0))].

As shown here, this graph is not in a particularly useful form, but it contains sufficient information to calculate an 8-point FFT, and can be readily transformed into machine instructions. Although there are 64 nodes in this graph, 16 of them are for holding constants, so it can be observed that only 48 additions and multiplications are required, by contrast to the 112 multiplications and additions needed if we were to evaluate the individual expressions given by the DFT.

It is possible to draw the above list in a more convenient graph form, in which each node is written as a circle enclosing an integer, representing one complex constant, one complex sum and one complex product, like this:

$$x + y \cdot \omega^k$$

With the coefficients written across the top of the graph as inputs, and the outputs appearing at the bottom, the above list is equivalent to the following:

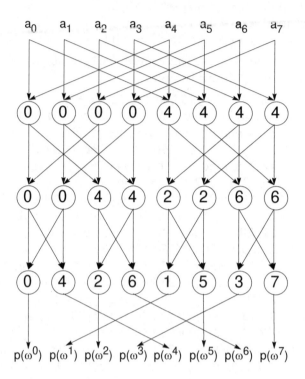

Here we can observe the beautiful 'butterfly' pattern characteristic of the data flow for the Fast Fourier Transform. What is remarkable is that the butterfly has been automatically derived: the pattern 'emerges' from the way that gen and eval produce their results. This can be contrasted to previous implementations of the FFT, in which it is necessary to explicitly program the sequence of data movements given by the butterfly pattern.

10.10 Bibliographic Notes

Standard methods for the DFT and FFT are reviewed in *Numerical Recipes*, by Press, W.H., Flannery, B.P., Teukolsky, S.A., and Vetterling W.T. (Cambridge University Press, 1988). The 'dataflow' method for deriving the FFT was invented by me, and was published in 1988 in *Journal of Logic Programming* **5**, 231-242. The clever way of using node was devised by my colleague Martin Richards. Standard methods for constructing DAGs can be found in *Principles of Compiler Design*, by Aho, A.V. and Ullman, J.D. (Addison-Wesley, 1977).

CHAPTER ELEVEN
CASE STUDY: HIGHER-ORDER
FUNCTIONAL PROGRAMMING

11.1 Introduction

Higher-order programming permits greater reuse of code and encourages the use of abstractions. This case study illustrates higher-order functional programming techniques in Prolog, and introduces new improvements to methods known to logic programmers for more than a decade. These are illustrated by defining an evaluator, written in Prolog, for higher-order functional programs.

One of the key advantages of programming in Prolog is the declarative reading possible for some programs, but it is not the only programming paradigm with this attribute. An alternative approach is to specify the desired computation as a collection of functions, and to obtain an answer through the functional evaluation of an expression representing the problem. For example, we could define a function that increments its argument in the following way using the following pseudocode:

fun inc(X) = X+1.

That is, the function 'inc' takes one argument (X) and returns the sum of X and 1. If we wish to find the 'inc' of 7, the expression inc(7) would be evaluated by substituting 7 for X, obtaining inc(7) = 7+1, or after further evaluation,

inc(7) = 8.

For another example, suppose that the list constructor is called cons, so that for the term cons(x,y), x is the head of the list and y is the tail. Then we may define a function hd to return the head of a list as follows:

fun hd(cons(X,Y)) = X.

and then we may have

    hd(cons(1,nil)) = 1.

These simple examples illustrate the three components of a functional program:

1. *Constructors*: the irreducible elements of the language such as integers and cons.

2. *Application*: the ability to apply a function to an argument, such as inc(7) and hd(cons(1,nil)).

3. *Abstraction*: giving a name to a function, such as naming inc the function defined by the lambda expression $\lambda x.x+1$. This expression means 'the function which, when applied to one argument, returns the incremented value of the argument'. The definition for inc shown above contains another function, namely '+' written in infix form, which can be assumed to be defined in a system library.

An important distinction between Prolog and most functional programming schemes is that the process of function evaluation is deterministic: that is, at each step of the execution of a functional program, only one possible evaluation step will be considered.

Functional programming extends very naturally to higher-order programming: the idea that functions can be given as arguments to other functions and returned as results. For example, consider a higher-order way of treating mapping. This is the same idea of mapping as we saw in Chapter 3. Here is a function called map that returns a list in which each element is the result of applying the input function to each element of the input list. There are two clauses: one to consider the empty list, and one to consider the list with head H and tail T:

    fun map(F, []) = [].
          map(F, [H|T]) = [F(H) | map(F, T)].

Here we use Prolog notation for lists. However, notice here that, unlike Prolog, it will be necessary to evaluate the functions given as the arguments of the list constructor (the F(H) and the map(F,T)).

So now if we use the inc function as defined above, and evaluate map(inc, [1,2,3]), we obtain

    map(inc, [1,2,3]) = [2,3,4]

This can be illustrated with the following box and arrows:

Many of the mappings we have seen in this book can be specified in terms of higher-order functions.

11.2 A Notation for Functions

To provide suitable facilities for exploring higher-order functional programming using Prolog, we require the following:

- Function expressions, called lambda expressions or λ-expressions. These are customarily denoted using the lambda operator λ, so that, for example, the lambda expression λx.x+1 is the function which, when applied to a number, returns the incremented value of the number. Here we shall use the term lambda(x,y), where x is a variable and y is a term representing the body of the function in which x is bound.

- Function application. The application of a function f to an argument x is usually denoted by juxtaposition, so for example f x. Sometimes one sees brackets used, for example f(x). To write function applications using Prolog syntax we shall declare the infix operator '@', so that f@x denotes a function application. Terms f and x evaluate to a function and an argument, respectively. Also, so that multiple arguments can be used, the list syntax will be always used to denote arguments, so for example, f@[x, y, z].

- Higher-order functions, as described above.

- Currying. This device[1] is to arrange that function applications of the form f@[x, y] are equivalent to f@[x]@[y]. This is useful in providing for function definitions that have more than one argument while preserving the conceptual viewpoint that all lambda expressions have only one argument. However, currying is more fundamental because it provides a means for ultimately dispensing with variables altogether.

In addition, we will assume that identifiers that cannot be reduced to a function value are assumed to be constructors – or, in Prolog nomenclature, functors of compound terms.

Functions are defined using the fun predicate, such that the clause fun(X,Y) defines the function named X having the definition Y. The function's name will also include a specification of its formal parameters represented as a Prolog list of variables. With the infix @

---

1. Attributed to M. Schönfinkel but named, perhaps to more mellifluous effect, after a pioneer of λ-calculus, Haskell Curry.

operator[1] denoting function application, we may define inc as:

    fun(inc@[X], sum@[X, 1]).

where sum is a built-in definition of a function that returns the sum of two numbers. We shall see later how to define built-in functions.
The list processing functions hd and tl may be defined as:

    fun(hd@[[X|_]], X).

    fun(tl@[[_|T]], T).

The standard Prolog syntax for lists is used.

   Boolean functions return either true or false. One useful function that makes use of boolean functions is the conditional – the 'if then else' – called 'if', which takes three arguments. The application if@[X,Y,Z] first evaluates X. If X evaluates to true, then the evaluation of Y is returned. If X is false, then the evaluation of Z is returned. It is important to know that depending on the value of the condition X, either Y or Z are evaluated, never both. This is useful in constructing expression such as

    if@[equal@[N, 0],
           X,
           quotient@[X, N]
       ]

where if N is zero, there is no way that the interpreter will divide by zero.

   Using the built-in arithmetic functions sum, difference and product, and the built-in equality function equal (which returns either true or false) we may define the factorial function as follows:

    fun(factorial@[N],
            if@[equal@[N, 1],
                   1,
                   product@[N, factorial@[difference@[N, 1]]]
               ]
).

List processing is illustrated by the concatenate function, which returns the concatenation of two lists:

---

1. For most Prolog systems it will be necessary to declare the infix operator with a directive such as :- op(600, yfx, '@').

```
fun(concatenate@[X, Y],
        if@[    equal@[X, []],
                Y,
                [ hd@[X] | concatenate@[tl@[X], Y] ]
            ]
    ).
```

Notice the use of the list notation to construct the list in the 'else' part of the if function. The higher-order function map is defined as follows:

```
fun(map@[F, L],
        if@[    equal@[L, []],
                [],
                [ F@[hd@[L]] | map@[F, tl@[L]] ]
            ]
    ).
```

The thing to notice here is the form F@... in the 'else' branch of the if application. Here a function passed as a parameter of map is applied to the head of the list. Being able to say 'F@' for a variable F illustrates one reason why higher-order functions are attractive.

The syntax of a functional programming language we have outlined here is perhaps not the most elegant, but it has the advantage of being expressed easily as a Prolog term, and thus easy to process by a Prolog program. Furthermore, using Prolog variables to stand for variables in the functional language confers a number of practical advantages, as we shall see.

11.3 The Evaluator

The next step is to define Prolog programs for evaluating functions such as those defined above. Let's begin with the built-in functions.

11.3.1 Built-in Functions

What is needed is an interface that will define the built-in functions in terms of a Prolog definition. Thus, a fun clause could be used, with the Prolog computation being done in the body of the clause. Here are definitions of some arithmetic functions done in this way:

```
fun(sum@[X,Y], Z) :- Z is X + Y.
fun(difference@[X,Y], Z) :- Z is X - Y.
fun(product@[X,Y], Z) :- Z is X * Y.
fun(equal@[X,X], true) :- !.
fun(equal@[_,_], false) :- !.
```

However, it is more useful if the second argument of fun clauses is written in the functional language rather than just using a Prolog variable. The way to do this is to use 'callouts', illustrated as follows:

```
fun(sum@[X,Y], callout@[sum,X,Y]).
fun(difference@[X,Y], callout@[difference,X,Y]).
fun(product@[X,Y], callout@[product,X,Y]).
fun(equal@[X,Y], callout@[equal,X,Y]).

callout(sum, X, Y, Z) :- Z is X + Y.
callout(difference, X, Y, Z) :- Z is X - Y.
callout(product, X, Y, Z) :- Z is X * Y.
callout(equal, X, X, true).
callout(equal, _, _, false).
```

These are called callouts because we are 'calling out' of the functional language evaluator into the native Prolog system to handle certain built-in functions. Below we shall arrange that the callouts are trapped by the evaluator, and the callout goal is satisfied to determine the result, which will pose as the result of the function definition. Because functions are deterministic, the evaluator will apply a 'cut' when a callout goal is satisfied, so it is not necessary to place a cut in the first callout clause for equal.

11.3.2 What Lambda Is For

The heart of the simulator is the evaluator. The eval predicate is defined such that for the goal eval(X,Y), the functional expression X is evaluated to determine the result Y. For this it is necessary to understand the role of lambda (introduced on page 127). When we define a function using fun, we are specifying that the value of the name of the function (and its formal parameters) is the definition of the function in terms of a function expression (or lambda expression). Suppose we use the clause val(X,Y) to say that the value of function name X is the lambda expression Y. Thus, the definition

```
fun(inc@[X], sum@[X,1])
```
is really saying

```
val(inc, lambda(X, sum@[X,1])).
```
Although the formal parameter, the Prolog variable X, no longer appears with the function name, it is given as the bound variable of the lambda expression.

Because lambda expressions (as defined here) bind only one variable, there is a question of what to do about functions with multiple arguments. This is what 'currying' is for. A lambda expression for each variable is simply nested within the body of another lambda expression, so there is one lambda expression for each formal parameter. Thus, the function definition

   fun(plus@[X, Y], sum@[X, Y])

is equivalent to

   val(plus, lambda(X, lambda(Y, sum@[X,Y]))).

And, correspondingly, the application

   plus@[3,4]

is equivalent to the applications

   plus@[3]@[4].

This is useful because it gives the opportunity to define functions in terms of other functions. For example, the function inc may be defined – without giving it an argument – as a curried version of the function plus, as follows:

   fun(inc, plus@[1]).

So whenever inc is applied to an argument, it is as though the function plus@[1] is applied to that argument, so

   inc@[7] = plus@[1]@[7] = plus@[1,7] = 8.

The 'uncurried' expression plus@[1,7] is shown here simply for illustrative purposes. There is actually no need to compute it. Although there is no real advantage to defining inc this way, consider the definition of inclist, which increments each element of a list:

   fun(inclist, map@[inc]).

This simple definition demonstrates the expressive power of higher-order functions and currying. Function inclist is defined as the function one obtains by applying map to inc. The second argument needed by map will be the argument to which inclist is applied. So now

   inclist@[[1,2,3]] = map@[inc]@[[1,2,3]] = map@[inc, [1,2,3]] = [2,3,4].

Again the 'uncurried' expression map@[inc, [1,2,3]] need not be computed if the curried equivalent is known.

11.3.3 The Evaluator

We are now in a position to give the Prolog clauses for eval. In the world of functional programming, eval is expected to handle variable bindings, normally by means of a parameter called the 'environment'. By contrast, the eval scheme offered here will use the underlying Prolog unification mechanism to handle variable binding, so there will be no need for environment parameters.

First consider the clause for evaluating applications of the form callout@[X,Y,Z], for dealing with built-in functions:

```
eval(callout@[Op,X,Y], Z) :-
        eval(X, X1),
        eval(Y, Y1),
        callout(Op, X1, Y1, Z), !.
```

This clause, together with the callout and fun clauses for the built-in functions defined above, constitutes the complete interface for built-in functions. The 'cut' ensures that evaluation is deterministic.

Next, consider the application of the 'if' function. First, we evaluate the condition, and then call an auxiliary function definition that selects which branch (the 'then' or the 'else' expression) to evaluate:

```
eval(if@[C,X,Y], Z) :-
        eval(C, C1),
        auxif(C1, X, Y, A),
        eval(A, Z), !.
```

where

```
auxif(true, X _, X).
auxif(false, _, X, X).
```

Again, the 'cut' ensures the determinacy of this evaluation step.

Now we should deal with atoms, which might be functions that evaluate to a lambda expression by virtue of a fun clause:

```
eval(F, Lx) :-
        atom(F),
        fun(F@X, Y),
        make_lambda(X, Y, Lx).
```

where make_lambda processes the formal parameter list, allowing for the possibility of multiple arguments:

```
make_lambda([], Y, Y).
make_lambda([X|Xs], Y, lambda(X,Z)) :- make_lambda(Xs, Y, Z).
```

Notice that if there is no function definition given by a fun clause, the eval clause fails, so the subsequent eval clauses may be tried (the atom will be considered to be a constructor).

The next case to consider is the application of a function expression to an argument. Because Prolog variables are being used as variables in our functional notation, it is necessary to rename the variables in a function definition each time the definition is used. Fortunately, the copy_term predicate, built into Standard Prolog, can be used to perform the renaming, and at the same time, perform the substitution of variables by values[1]:

```
eval(Fx@[A], Z) :-
        eval(Fx, Lx),
        eval(A, A1),
        copy_term(Lx, lambda(A1, Y)),
        eval(Y, Z), !.
```

The function expression is evaluated first so that failure can happen early if the function has no definition. Then the argument is evaluated, then the copy and substitution takes place, then the resulting expression is evaluated. The more general case of multiple arguments simply recurs on eval for each argument, nesting each lambda expression within the next one, again showing the elegance of processing curried notation:

```
eval(Fx@[A|As], Z) :-
        eval(Fx, Lx),
        eval(A, A1),
        copy_term(Lx, lambda(A1, Y)),
        eval(Y@As, Z), !.
```

If an application is not a function application, then we assume it is an application:

```
eval(C@L, C@L1) :- eval(L, L1), !.
```

Next we evaluate the list constructor notation, which is a contructor in its own right, as well as being needed by the previous clause to evaluate the argument list of a constructor:

```
eval([X|Xs], [Y|Ys]) :- eval(X, Y), eval(Xs, Ys), !.
```

It is useful to use tuple notation, so here is a similar clause to handle tuples (simply the ',' constructor suitably bracketed):

```
eval((X,Xs), (Y,Ys)) :- eval(X, Y), eval(Xs, Ys), !.
```

Finally, the 'catchall', so that any other terms (such as 1 and true) evaluate to themselves:

```
eval(X, X).
```

The above clauses constitute the evaluator.

---

1. This amounts to doing both of what practitioners of functional programming call α-conversion and β-conversion.

11.4 Using Higher-Order Functions

Let's look at some general-purpose higher-order functions that can be evaluated by the above evaluator. We have already seen map, which returns a list in which a function has been applied to each member of the input list. The map function embodies the abstract pattern of what we called the 'full map' in the worksheets. Many of the full maps in the worksheets may be redefined in a functional style using map. For example, from Worksheet 10, we can define sqlist in terms of map and square:

   fun(sqlist, map@[square]).

   fun(square@[X], product@[X,X]).

Not only this, but because we treat undefined functions as constructors, we can define the envelope function of Worksheet 10 as:

   fun(envelope, map@[container]).

Because container is not defined as a function, we treat it as a constructor, so

   envelope@[[1,2,3]] = [container@[1], container@[2], container@[3]].

Indeed, because full mapping is inherently deterministic, using map in a functional language is perhaps a better fit to the problem than using Prolog, whose nondeterminism is more powerful than is needed for the problem.

   Another useful function is foldl, which embodies the pattern of a valuation (page 27) using an accumulator (page 22). The foldl function is given a function, an initial value of the accumulator, and a list. On each recurrence, the function (which must take two arguments) is applied to the accumulator and the next element of the list, with the result being the new accumulator. For example, we may express a factorial function by 'folding' product along a list of suitably chosen integers, initialising the accumulator to 1. :

   foldl@[product, 1, [1,2,3,4,5,6]] = 720.

Knowing about currying gives the hint that factorial may be defined as:

   fun(factorial, foldl@[product, 1]).

so that

   factorial@[1,2,3,4,5,6] = 720.

The name foldl means 'fold from the left'. We may define foldl as follows:

```
fun(foldl@[F, A, L]
        if@[    equal@[L, []],
                A,
                foldl@[F, F@[A, hd@[L]], tl@[L]]
        ]
    ).
```

Folding 'from the left' captures the tail-recursive formulation of the equivalent Prolog program in the worksheet. It is also possible to write a foldr function, which folds 'from the right' of the list, defined as follows:

```
fun(foldr@[F, A, L]
        if@[    equal@[L, []],
                A,
                F@[hd@[L], foldr@[F, A, tl@[L]]
        ]
    ).
```

It is instructive to compare the evaluation of the above definition of factorial with a version using foldr instead of foldl.

Sometimes it is useful to initialise the accumulator from an element of the input list. The higher-order function fold, which is not defined for the empty list, does this:

```
fun(fold@[F, L]
        if@[    equal@[L, [A]],
                A,
                F@[hd@[L], fold@[F, tl@[L]]
        ]
    ).
```

So, assuming there is a built-in function max that returns the maximum of two numeric arguments, a function to find the maximum element of a list may be expressed as folding max along a list follows:

```
fold@[max]@[3,1,4,1,5,9,2,6] = 9.
```

Notice the use of curried notation, which gives the hint that we could define

```
fun(maxlist, fold@[max]).
```

so that

```
maxlist@[2,7,1,8,2,8] = 8.
```

Partial maps (page 32) may be implemented with the higher-order function filter. The filter function is given a boolean 'guard' function and a list. The result is a list of all the elements in the input list that satisfy the guard. For example, assuming there is a built-in function mod(x,y), which returns the remainder when x is divided by y, we can find all the even members of an input list as follows:

fun(iseven@[X], equal@[mod@[X,2], 0]).

filter@[iseven]@[1,2,3,4,5] = [2,4].

Similarly, accompanied by a function to test list membership, filter could be used to define a higher-order functional version of setify (page 33).

11.5 Discussion

The higher-order functional style of programming encourages more concise programs through more abstraction. Prolog provides a unique way to explore these topics because of the convenience of using unification of logical variables and writing evaluators. To gain the theoretical advantages of higher-order functional programming, it is not necessary to change Prolog in any way, although using a purpose-designed functional language such as Miranda or ML will have the practical advantages of appropriate syntax, more language features, and computational efficiency.

This case study has covered the main features of higher-order programming, but there are a number of further topics that have not been explored. One is the composition of functions. You might wish to express a function which has the effect of applying f to an argument x, then applying g to the result, that is $g(f(x))$. This can be done by introducing the function composition $g°f$ and applying $(g°f)(x)$. In this way, the benefits of currying are apparent, as we may define

fun(h, g*f)

where the infix * operator is used to denote function composition, and then saying

h@[X]

in place of

g@[f@[X]].

It is not difficult to introduce function composition into the evaluator, and this is given as one of the exercises below.

Another topic is how to handle free variables, that is, variables in a λ-expression that are not bound. For example, in the λ-expression

lambda(X, lambda(Y, sum@[X, sum@[Y,Z]]))

the variable Z is free. Our simulator ignores free variables. If a free variable appears in a lambda expression, it is an anonymous variable, with no chance of being unified with anything. This is because of the specific structure of our interpreter. In a practical functional programming system, one way to handle free variables is to evaluate variables in the context of an environment of variable bindings.

A third topic we have not discussed is types. Types are a major issue for practitioners of functional programming. However, the evaluator defined above resides within the conventions of Prolog, which is concerned with the unification of terms rather than the specification of types. The definitions of the mapping, folding, and filtering higher-order functions given above make no particular commitment to the kind of terms given as elements of the input lists, and so these functions can be considered polymorphic. Of course, there is no checking whether the input functions are type-compatible with the contents of the input lists.

Exercises

1. In the definition of fold above, which element of the input list is chosen to initialise the accumulator?
2. Define a folding function fold2r that can be used to define the inner product of two vectors represented as lists, in the manner of Worksheet 7.
3. Define a higher-order functional version of setify as suggested above.
4. Augment the evaluator to provide the built-in functions mod and max.
5. Augment the evaluator to handle function composition.
6. Augment the evaluator to give a sensible interpretation of free variables.

11.6 Bibliographic Notes

A good introduction to functional programming is *Miranda: The Craft of Functional Programming*, by Simon Thompson (Addison Wesley, 1995). A more advanced treatment is given in *ML for the Working Programmer*, by L.C. Paulson (Cambridge University Press, 1991).

The need for this case study is paralleled by the recent paper 'Higher-order programming in Prolog', by Lee Naish (Technical Report 96/2, Department of Computer Science, University of Melbourne, Australia), which discusses various techniques that have been proposed for supporting higher-order programming in Prolog. These involve introducing Prolog predicates call/N and apply. There is an active debate concerning the relative merits of these and other techniques which Naish reviews.

However, the approach taken in this case study, which is based on work done with my colleague Ian Lewis, is to use abstract interpretation, making explicit use of λ-expressions and an explicit syntactic device for denoting function application (the @ operator). The reason we take this approach is because our main concern is not primarily with higher-order logic programming. Although our approach is not the most computationally efficient, we believe it to be a satisfying way to reveal the principles exploited by higher-order functional programming within a logic programming context.

Index

Springer
and the
environment

At Springer we firmly believe that an international science publisher has a special obligation to the environment, and our corporate policies consistently reflect this conviction.
We also expect our business partners – paper mills, printers, packaging manufacturers, etc. – to commit themselves to using materials and production processes that do not harm the environment. The paper in this book is made from low- or no-chlorine pulp and is acid free, in conformance with international standards for paper permanency.

 Springer

Printing: Saladruck, Berlin
Binding: Buchbinderei Lüderitz & Bauer, Berlin